ROGUES, RASCALS, AND SCALAWAGS TOO

More Brazen Ne're-Do-Wells Through the Ages

Other books by Jim Christy

The Price of Power
(a biography of Charles Bedaux)

Flesh and Blood
(a study of professional boxing)

The Redemption of Anna Dupree (novel)

Nine O'Clock Gun (novel)

Tight Like That (stories)

Cavatinas (poetry)

God's Little Angle (a CD of poetry and songs)

*Scalawags: Rogues, Roustabouts, Wags & Scamps
—Brazen Ne'er-Do-Wells Through the Ages*

The Big Thirst and Other Doggone Poems

ROGUES, RASCALS, AND SCALAWAGS TOO

More Brazen Ne're-Do-Wells
Through the Ages

JIM CHRISTY

anvil
PRESS

Anvil Press Publishers Inc.
P.O. Box 3008, Main Post Office
Vancouver, B.C. V6B 3X5 CANADA
www.anvilpress.com

Library and Archives Canada Cataloguing in Publication

Christy, Jim, 1945-, author
    Rogues, rascals, and scalawags too : more ne'er-do-wells
through the ages / Jim Christy.

ISBN 978-1-77214-017-0 (pbk.)

    1. Rogues and vagabonds—Biography. 2. Rogues and vagabonds—
History. I. Title.

CT9980.C472 2015   364.1092'2   C2015-901622-3

Book design by Derek von Essen
Cover images: (l to r) TOP: Mata Hari, Bata Kindai Amgoza ibn LoBagola,
William Leonard Hunt (The Great Farini); BOTTOM: Carolina Otéro
Author photo by John Hamley

Represented in Canada by the Publishers Group Canada
Distributed by Raincoast Books

The publisher gratefully acknowledges the financial assistance of the Canada Council for the Arts, the Canada Book Fund, and the Province of British Columbia through the B.C. Arts Council and the Book Publishing Tax Credit.

"Lovers and madmen have such seething brains,
Such shaping fantasies, that apprehend
More than cool reason ever comprehends."
     —William Shakespeare, *A Midsummer Night's
     Dream*

"The extraordinary seems ordinary to me because I don't
see what's so extraordinary about it."
     —Momo, in *Madame Rosa* by Émile Ajar,
     widely known as Romain Gary, but also known
     as Shatan Bogart, a.k.a. Fosco Sinibaldi, a.k.a.
     Robert Markham, who was born Roman Kacew,
     but could have been born Simon Katcheff, either
     in Vilna, Russian Empire, or Kraków, Poland.
     No one knows. He is also the only person ever to
     win the Prix Goncourt twice, which is against the
     rules. But he's another story.

To Chris Faiers and Morley Ellis
and the Count, wherever he is.

Table of Malcontents

About the Author

Foreword

As if the scale of Christy's exploration into the world of the bizarre and the extraordinary in *Scalawags: Rogues, Roustabouts, Wags & Scamps—Brazen Ne'er-Do-Wells Through the Ages* was not remarkable enough, he has now come up with over thirty more equally astonishing oddities in the twenty-six chapters of this wonderfully illustrated follow-up. As with the first volume of *Scalawags*, what makes the lives of this parade of rascals so irresistible, is that they represent a world that is lost to us forever. Not that there are no 21st Century scoundrels, but internet fraud just doesn't evoke the romance and excitement of voyaging around the globe while assuming exotic personas and smooth-talking your way into the confidence, and the beds, of the rich and famous. By comparison with today's bland diet of manufactured movie and TV celebrities that daily assaults and insults our senses, these heroic adventurers of the past are a real inspiration to just how much can be realized and accomplished out of one life in spite of all the odds. O.K., some of them caused other people misery too, but as Nietzsche recognized, that is the price we pay for being human, all too human. What the following pages offer is more superhuman, and at times even magical.

Even while researching those better known scoundrels, what Christy brings to this book is an eye for the oddball, the absurd, and the quirky facts that are otherwise overlooked. As a vagabond himself, Christy has a special affinity with much of the world inhabited in this book. Sometime gangster (of the benevolent, Robin Hood kind), hobo, pugilist, circus roustabout, bit-part actor, private eye, music promoter, sports writer, and much more, he understands well the parlance of those who exist in the margins, and is attracted to them in the same way that some of those featured in this book were attracted to him. Bill Caradine, "Uncle Bull," was a minor fraudster and con man who married Christy's aunt and had an influence on the young Christy before disappearing on to his next caper. Christy also introduces us to his one-time partner in crime, eighty-year-old movie actor, architect and fraudster, Jack Donovan. Several more "characters" known to Christy are mentioned in the final chapter.

The only talent Christy does not share with this roll call of incorrigibles, in spite of his powerful imagination and outlandish adventures, is that he himself does not indulge in lies and exaggerations, it is just not in his style. He has a modesty that many of the other scalawags featured here did not. If anything, Christy plays down his adventures and is embarrassed about mentioning them, precisely because—a recurring theme of this book—those with mundane lives insist on questioning the validity of those whose lives are remarkable; unless, of course, those lives are recorded in the "history books," which is where one finds the biggest lies of all.

Christy claims in his introduction that his aim in writing this book is to rescue these scalawags from oblivion, from the trash can of history; he even insists that he is performing a public service by doing so, something I would entirely endorse. Herbert Dyce Murphy and Edward John Trelawny, are just two of those whose stories were not believed, even though in Murphy's case he was more of a hero (and sometime heroine) than a scalawag. But, as with André Malraux, featured in the first chapter, enhancing the fiction about oneself can actually intensify the mystique and notoriety of the individual, especially when their real life is more remarkable and infamous than their fictional life. And so when Malraux's doubters start prying in order to expose what they regard as lies or exaggerations, what they will uncover are even more remarkable truths. Others, like Edward James, have left physical legacies of their crazy dreams that can still be seen today by those adventurous enough to seek them out.

But for his modesty, Christy would have been justified in including himself in this inventory of rapscallions. In any case, his own life story is well documented elsewhere. But Christy's scalawag provenance—well, more full-blown outlaw—is itself remarkable. Real name Christinzio, on his father's side Christy's family were ward bosses in a corrupt Philadelphia political machine having previously left Molise in Italy under a dark cloud. Christy's godfather was the "Gentle Don," Angelo Bruno, actual Godfather of the Philadelphia/South Jersey/Delaware branch of a fabled organized crime family that Christy always insists on not naming. On his mother's side he is related to the cattle-rustling Clantons, murdered by the Earps in the now legendary "Gunfight at the OK Corral."

What makes those featured in this book stand out is that they took chances in life, but also, like Christy himself, crammed more living into their (sometimes short) lives than several dozen ordinary mortals can do combined, and some, like Stephen Weinberg, lived several different lives simultaneously. They either shared an exaggerated imagination and belief in themselves, one that often brought enormous rewards, or were hugely talented but self-deprecating. Importantly, for true scalawag status, the acquisition of goods or money for its own sake was not the principal motivator. For many it was the thrill and pleasure of the scam itself, something that often also enriched and gave pleasure to others. Most of those featured on the following pages were charismatic in one way or another (Frederick Emerson Peters even charmed his jailers) and many, both men and women, also exploited their sexual charms. Here we have eccentric aristocrats, the poverty stricken made good (some by attaching themselves to aristocrats as did certain courtesans such as La Belle Otero), extremes of entrepreneurship, delusions of grandeur such as Timothy Dexter, or just plain thieving, bullshitting con artists who took the art of trickery to remarkable extremes— like Victor Lustig who sold the Eiffel Tower to a scrap merchant. Then there are loveable cool cats like Harry "the hipster" Gibson who was imitated and overshadowed by much less talented musicians, but had a hell of a time anyway. I defy anyone to read this book without—for different reasons—having their favourites whose lives and exploits they will be compelled to delve into and explore further.

— Ian Cutler, author of *Cynicism from Diogenes to Dilbert*

Introduction

Upon looking over the contents of this second volume of scalawagish characters, I am gratified to see that they are just as audacious and just as imbued with the old derring-do as the first bunch, if not more so. I had thought there were no rogues in any gallery who could out-adventure that lot. Some of them are frankly larcenous, many libidinous, and all completely lacking in any predilection for a conventional life. It's not as if they show contempt for the day-to-day round, but rather such a thing was never considered. It wasn't, as so many are fond of saying in these parlous times of group speak, an "option" —especially not a career option, not even as temporary refuge. Like their predecessors they were possessed by that intense rage to live, however it may have manifested itself in their too brief times.

I have to laugh over the two reviews of the previous *Scalawags* that declared the book a work of fiction, one review being titled "Tall Tales." Well, they were an outsized lot, head and shoulders above the average or, for that matter, the dull crooks in the news so much for having perpetrated monstrous frauds at the expense of hapless victims. And *Too* is too.

I regard these reviews and the comments of those who have taken me aside and said, "You made them up, didn't you? You can tell me," as an affirmation of my intent and my research.

I knew a few of the subjects in *Too*; I am in fact sort of related to one of them. So it is "personal" this time.

Fiction! As if I could have made up—or you could have either— Bata Kindai Amgoza ibn LoBagola!

All the essays in *Scalawags*, and many of those in the current volume, were written for a certain glossy, quarterly magazine. But after eleven years and all too soon, for me, our relationship came to an end. None of these scalawags are alive now, although one of them seems simply to have disappeared. Of course, in a time when so many now have no interest in what happened last week, one might ask, Who cares? Well, this book provides an answer.

So involved was I, so absorbed in the pursuit of these rogues and rascals, that I could not stop pursuing them. After the column's demise, I kept collecting, rescuing rascals from oblivion, and I intend to continue exploring the obscure realms, the byways and backwaters, of history searching for figures in the shadows. I believe that I am not only indulging myself, but doing a public service by bringing these folks to light and holding them up as examples of how the world was not so long ago, when a person was not hemmed in by security. "The woods are full of wardens," said Mr. Kerouac in antediluvian times (the mid-fifties). How quaint that comment seems in light of the present homogenized era—nothing less than a security state—we live in. Instead of wardens who were actual human beings, there are now video cameras in the crotches of trees, microphone buds in the very buds, and drones above the forest canopy.

But forget that for a while. Let us now return to former days, glory days, of skulduggery and swashbuckling, days of bedsheet prison escapes, stowaway girls dressed as boys; when you could find a million-dollar baby in a five-and-ten-cent store, catch a tramp and convince the captain to go off course and visit that fabled isle of notorious dancing girls who just love visitors (or, for that matter, convince him to call at the one with the dancing boys —*whatever*).

I have it on good authority—my old friend Marcel Horne— that every year in another realm, the one to which he himself has retired, the great rogues and rascals of times past get together at the tomb of Constantine Rafinesque and drink a toast to those imbued with the wrong stuff, never forgetting to spill a few ceremonial drops on the ground in their honour. So now I raise my own glass to them: I salute you one and all. Perhaps you inhabit that great Wire Store of Heaven. May all your horses come from behind like the immortal Silky Sullivan, and may there be vast celestial Floridas of underwater lots and the marks to buy them; may there be doubloons in your gutters and Double Eagles in a perpetual pearly blue sky.

One last thing: I want to thank all those who sent in their money orders for the *Scalawags* course, complete with disguises. There are

still a few left, but with an added feature: a beard of genuine—
would I kid you?—yak hair, plus a special, free, bonus Belizean
passport (I actually once carried one of these, but that's another
story). Unfortunately, the price has been raised to $59.95, to reflect
the reality of doing business in these times. Order now. All sales
are final, and you will not be bothered by robocalls; we're
scalawags, after all, not politicians.

—Jim Christy

André Malraux
1901–1976

In the introduction to *Scalawags,* I had a bit of fun at the expense of the august André Malraux, long gone into the Pantheon. I wouldn't have dared had he been alive for fear of being smote while bedazzled by Malrucian verbiage. Anyway, I wrote that this unblushing teller of whoppers boasted of his long friendship with Chairman Mao, and this presumed association lead to his being summoned to brief Richard Nixon prior to the president's historic trip to China. Well I was wrong. The two men had met, as we shall see. But there are enough other lies to more than make up for it, and most of what he told Nixon was a lie anyway.

Also in that introduction, I declared that Malraux did not warrant scalawag status, although he was awfully close. In that pronouncement, I was, as further investigation has revealed, very much mistaken. There is simply no precedent for André Malraux.

IMAGE: Andre Malraux with windswept hair and cigarette, Paris (1935) by Gisèle Freund.

Others may have told bigger whoppers—*maybe*—but he lied on such a grand scale and on such a vast stage—the world stage—that one can only marvel at his audacity and be frankly awestruck that he got away with it.

But there was much, much more to André Malraux than his fabrications and his self-glorification. All his lies were an extension of his vision of himself; his stories had at their centre the man he wanted to be. And the strange thing is that unlike many other famous mythomaniacs—Ernest Hemingway, for instance—there was a real hero in there, and not always so far below the surface.

Malraux was born in 1901, into a lower-middle-class family in the suburbs of Paris. His parents split up when he was six years old and he was raised by his mother and aunt above a confectioner's shop. An indifferent student, Malraux quit school and went to live in Paris, supporting himself by roaming the stands of *bouquinistes* along the quays, buying rare items to be resold at a profit. He also dabbled in small publishing projects, chiefly art reproductions, and read widely about the history of world art. Having come across information that Khmer art sold well, he determined to go to Cambodia and get some of it. For that he needed money, and he found the money in the dowry of Clara Goldschmidt, a woman two years his senior whom he married.

Malraux spent an intense month or so studying the art of Southeast Asia and signing deals to sell art he hadn't yet acquired. Malraux, Clara, and a friend, Louis Chevasson, arrived in Saigon before travelling on to Phnom Penh in Cambodia. They went to the small ceremonial site of Banteay Srei, fifty kilometres from the vast, and vastly more famous, Angkor Wat. This is important to note because Banteay Srei was not known to tourists, therefore, their plan could unfold away from prying eyes. The idea was to liberate several friezes from the stone wherein they had been ensconced for hundreds of years. In other words, under Malraux's direction they robbed the ancient ceremonial site. Having been to Banteay Srei, I can testify that this was a devastating and audacious desecration of a prime example of the glories of Khmer culture.

Malraux might have been audacious but he was not exactly, at this point, worldly. The haughtiness that he would display for the rest of his life prevented him from paying the necessary bribes and the three foreigners were arrested before their chartered boat could sail. After they had been held under house arrest for a couple of months, Clara was released and hurried to Paris to politic on Malraux's behalf. It worked. Clara got a passel of important writers to sign a petition for his release, claiming he was such an important writer— never mind that his literary résumé was comprised of only three published essays—that it would be a crime to keep him in prison for ten years. Finally, he was let go. One can only wonder what would have happened to him had he not been declared to have a brilliant literary future.

Anyway, Malraux was back in Paris for only two months before he and Clara left again for Southeast Asia where, in Saigon, he and a partner started an anticolonial newspaper. It was tolerated by the authorities for a year.

Again in Paris, he wrote his first novel, *Les Conquérants* (about revolution in China, a country he had never visited), and had his first success. He found a job with the publisher Gallimard, but couldn't fight off the demon of travel and the lust for art hustling. With the support of the NRF gallery in Paris, Malraux and Clara departed from Marseille on a steamer to tour the Middle East, acquiring, mainly from shops, local art objects and paintings. This was strictly a tourist trip, with regular scheduled trains and hired drivers. After three months, back in Paris, Malraux arranged an exhibit of this work as an advertisement for sales. A columnist for *Comoedia* remarked to Malraux that he must have special skills to relate to local people and acquire such fine pieces, to which Malraux nodded and replied, "I know Sanskrit and I'm studying Persian."

When the journalist further said that the trip must have been quite dangerous, Malraux agreed: "Outside of Kabul, an expedition would need machine guns. For me, it's not the same, I was a commissar in Canton...the armed nomads of the Pamir recognize a man who can handle a revolver or a machine gun."

A few months later, the couple was off to Russia, India, and Japan, sponsored by the gallery and travelling first class.

Soon Malraux began dabbling in Communism, which he interrupted in 1934 to fly to the Middle East, having announced he was looking for Marib, the Lost City of the Queen of Sheba. In Yemen, he and his two companions flew over some ruins and their plane was fired on, ineffectually, by Berber tribesmen. Malraux was thrilled. He pronounced the ruins to be those of the Queen of Sheba's Marib. His find has never been supported by a single archaeologist.

The next year, when Trotsky was sent to prison in Kazakhstan, Malraux wrote to three adventurous writer friends, Joseph Kessler, Blaise Cendrars, and Pierre Mac Orlan, proposing the four of them embark on an expedition to rescue Trotsky. He got no takers.

But it was in 1936 that Malraux began his genuine heroics. He found airplanes for Spain after the Republic government was attacked by General Franco. In exchange, he was made a lieutenant colonel and given command of a squadron, a mix of adventurers and mercenaries who dressed in sombreros and cowboy boots. With this crew, Malraux flew twenty-three missions as a tail gunner. In 1938, while under siege in Catalonia, he, along with Boris Peskine, directed the film *Sierra de Teruel*, adapted from Malraux's novel *L'Espoir* about the Spanish Civil War.

He didn't volunteer for duty when the Second World War broke out, but was drafted in 1940 as a reserve. He could have easily avoided service but used his influence to enter under a pseudonym and be a foot soldier. After the fall of France, Malraux spent two years of lavish domesticity in the Riviera with his new lover, Josette Clotis.

He didn't join the Resistance until 1944. Calling himself Colonel Berger, the following year was one of clandestine movie lore, complete with dangerous missions, imprisonment, and escapes. Much of this was true, or somewhat true. What cannot be denied is that Colonel Berger and the nearly two thousand men under him, known as the Brigade Alsace-Lorraine, engaged elite German troops in several battles, including that of Strasbourg.

After the war, Malraux was awarded the Croix de guerre and picked by Charles de Gaulle to serve as cultural adviser and, subsequently, in de Gaulle's two administrations, 1945–46 and 1958–69, as minister for information and minister of cultural affairs, respectively. In this latter position, he implemented his program of *maisons de la culture*, which would establish in every département of France a centre to present all forms of culture to the citizenry. He also had all the grand buildings of Paris sandblasted. Most significantly, however, Malraux travelled the world as a sort of booster of French culture. In Washington in 1962, he met the Kennedys, and Jackie fell for him. As a spontaneous gesture to her, an equally smitten Malraux offered to send the Mona Lisa on a visit to the United States. This gesture, which he had no authority to make, horrified French diplomats and de Gaulle himself, but it turned out to be a major success.

When de Gaulle died, Malraux's world began to crumble. He did, however, turn a brief deathbed conversation with the general to one of his best books, *The Fallen Oaks*, wherein he claimed they spoke for several hours, as equals, about the way the world was going and how it had gone.

After de Gaulle's death, Malraux became gravely ill and was in hospital or convalescence for nearly a year. When Malraux emerged, he was pale, feeble, and, some said, near death. It so happens that at this time the Bengalis rebelled in India. Malraux declared he would go and fight alongside the Bengali rebels. Not only that, the seventy-year-old invalid would raise a foreign legion which he would command. This romantic delusion had him in its grip for several months until Indira Gandhi disabused him of the notion.

It was in February, 1972, that President Nixon invited him to Washington because Malraux had known Mao and Chou En-lai and others since the 1930s. In truth, Malraux, as a sort of a travelling salesman for Gaullism, had met the Great Leader for a few minutes. Although he was in the same room as Mao for an hour, much of this time was taken up with ceremonial introductions and in pausing for translations. The transcript and notes indicate that the two men spoke for fifteen minutes. The next day, in Hong Kong, he told the world press when he alighted from the airplane that he and his old comrade had passed three hours in the deepest, most serious conversation. He didn't mention translators because as everyone should know, he, Malraux, had graduated from the Institute of Oriental Languages in Paris. Which was, of course, also not true.

In Washington, during a two-hour meeting and dinner that night, Malraux provided Nixon and his aides with all they needed to know about China and the psychology and personal habits of their Great Leader. Most of the throng, Nixon especially, was taken in by Malraux's act. It was as if Malraux was the teacher and Nixon the acolyte. Henry Kissinger later declared, "It was a stunning performance."

Malraux divided the last four years of his life between travelling, being honoured—receiving the Gandhi Award in India and being treated like a founder in Bangladesh—and writing. He died in 1976, and twenty years later his ashes were interred in the Panthéon in Paris. That year, 1996, Malraux was everywhere: in biographies, posters in the subways, photographs in magazines; there was even a Malraux fashion craze featuring berets and trench coats.

He wrote at least one great book, *L'Espoir*, and co-directed one great film, *Sierra de Teruel*. How many have done that much? But more than most writers, his work and his life cannot be separated. His mythomania is difficult to condemn because he was partly that person he believed himself to be. From childhood, he was consumed by a romantic and dramatic vision of himself and as he aged, Malraux only became more consumed by it. So much so that even his closest friends, who might have known the facts, nevertheless bought the legend which was of course not just a legend. As his mates on that bomber in Spain said, "Malraux had balls." What other trickster has gotten away with that?

Emma Hamilton
1765–1815

Consider the young hooker leaning against a lamppost in London's Soho district in 1778. The girl, Amy Lyon, had somehow managed to survive all odds to reach the age of thirteen. Her father, a blacksmith, died when she was a month old; after her mother fled to London, Amy was brought up by grandparents. Her diet consisted of bread, potatoes, and lard, and she was happy to get that. She worked from the time she was old enough to carry a bucket. At age eleven, she escaped to the big city. There she toiled for room and meagre board at one house after another, before hitting the street.

Consider Emma Hamilton at age twenty-six, wife of the Queen's envoy to the Court of Naples, the most beautiful and famous English woman of her time—accomplished dancer, singer, spy, fashion plate, and mistress to Lord Nelson, England's greatest hero.

Consider that they are the same woman.

IMAGE: *Lady Hamilton as Circe* painting by George Romney. *Image © Tate, London 2012.*

Amy wasn't on the street for long before being enlisted into high-class brothels. Painters of the day toured such establishments looking for models. Sir Joshua Reynolds took one look at the thirteen-year-old and offered her work. Now calling herself Emily, she was Reynolds's model for *Cupid Untying the Zone of Venus*.

Still only thirteen, Emily was hired by the eccentric James Graham, owner of the notorious Temple of Health, where she danced provocatively while he gave lectures on sex and electricity. She graduated to work in the newly opened Temple of Hymen at Schomberg House in Pall Mall, wherein reposed Graham's Celestial Bed, advertised as promising potency, ecstasy, and healthy babies. It was a large contraption with purple satin sheets, canopied by a dome covered in musical automata, and elevated on glass pillars in a mirrored room with crystal chandeliers, and fake stained-glass windows. While couples were aspiring to ecstasy, Emily danced privately for them wearing practically nothing.

Emily was soon the star of the joint, and by the time she was recruited by Madame Kelly to work in her exclusive bordello, she was well established as a legend of the *demi-monde*, her recruitment being noted in *Town and Country* magazine.

Madame Kelly's girls could be rented for extended periods of time, and thus Emily became the temporary property of Sir Harry Fetherstonhaugh, known around high-class brothels as Sir Flagellum. He originally took Emily for a month, but kept her for a year, until she became pregnant and he threw her out in the street. She was taken in by one of his friends, Sir Charles Greville, but the baby was sent away immediately. Greville got the idea that he could earn good commissions by hiring her out to painters. Emily would pose for artists the rest of her life. Art historians claim that no other European woman in history has been painted as often.

Greville kept Emily cooped up in a house on the edge of town where she soon grew bored. Tired of her complaining, Greville sent her off to his uncle, Sir William Hamilton, British Envoy to Naples, a cultured fifty-five-year-old collector of antiquities. Emily was expected to charm him, and the grateful Hamilton would be disposed to leave his estate to Greville. The woman the magazines called "the prettiest girl in England" arrived in Naples the day of her twenty-first birthday. Hamilton arranged for her to have music and language lessons. Artists begged to paint her, and people lined up outside Hamilton's villa for a look at her. She was soon his mistress.

He had noticed her posing before mirrors and Emily explained that she was "assuming attitudes," often scenes from classical mythology. The envoy began to feature her as an after-dinner act at the villa, singing and doing her attitudes, which were actually a continuation of her brothel posing of former days. Upon seeing her, Johann Wolfgang von Goethe, the most famous writer of his day, remarked, "A spectator can hardly believe his eyes." He later featured her in his novel *Elective Affinities,* as did Madame de Staël in *Corinne ou l'Italie.*

Changing her name to Emma, she was married to Sir William Hamilton in a secret ceremony in England. On their honeymoon tour she became friends with Marie Antoinette, sister of Queen Carolina of the Kingdom of Naples, and a confidante of Emma. In January, 1793, King Louis XVI was executed and in February, France declared war on England. Back in Naples, Hamilton received news that French troops were headed his way, and a messenger from the navy was bringing news and a request for troops to engage the French at Toulon. The messenger was Captain Horatio Nelson, who took one look at Emma and that, as they say, was all she wrote.

Back in England, Nelson's wife Fanny fretted because he was to meet the woman the newspapers said, "no man can resist." Theirs was a childless, miserable marriage, but the daring captain didn't have time to surrender to Emma's charms. It was she who interceded with the king and queen to get Nelson his men and supplies. Emma was soon working for the British government passing along information about the royal court and about travellers and spies.

Again, a year later, it was Emma who arranged for Nelson's ships to be supplied so that he could go on to the Battle of the Nile and the victory that made him the greatest hero in English history. By the time he returned to Naples, Nelson had lost an eye and an arm. He collapsed in Emma's two arms as he disembarked from his ship, both of them hopelessly in love. A resigned Hamilton offered the hero

a place in his household. The three of them would live together—
except when Nelson was at sea—until the end of Hamilton's life.

It is difficult to realize these days how famous and respected
Nelson was. His image was everywhere: people dressed *à la Nelson*,
and decorated their homes in the same fashion. But in civilian garb,
Nelson could walk down the street unnoticed because he didn't
look the part. He was no more than five foot two and not handsome.
In uniform, and with Emma, they stopped traffic, but after the initial
shock of recognizing the hero, people switched their attention to
Lady Hamilton. She looked like the "Goddess of the World," according
to one Italian diplomat. "It is like seeing Cleopatra in the flesh."

Nelson, with Emma and Hamilton aboard, put down a rebellion
that saved the king and queen of Naples from being overthrown,
and Emma on her own initiative sent funds to Malta to rescue the
country from being overrun by rebels. She became the first woman
to receive the Maltese Cross.

The three proceeded on a triumphant tour of Europe. They
arrived in England in November, 1800, where Emma, seven months
pregnant with Nelson's child, met his wife. A deluded and desperate
Fanny demanded Nelson choose between her and Emma. He never
saw his wife again.

On January 29, 1801, while Nelson was on duty, Emma gave
birth to a daughter whom she named Horatia. He stole time to write
dozens of letters that display his thorough sexual obsession with
the former courtesan.

After a dubious victory at the Battle of Copenhagen and service
off the south coast of England, Nelson was able to return to Emma.
They moved into Merton Place, a small house near Wimbledon, where
Nelson, Emma, Hamilton, and Emma's mother all lived. Sir William
Hamilton died in April, 1803, in Emma's arms while Nelson held
his hand.

Whatever Emma was left by Hamilton went to creditors. In early
1804, while Nelson was away, she gave birth to another daughter
who lived only six weeks. Nelson returned after two years and was
home only a month before leaving. He was killed off the north coast
of Spain in what came to be known as the Battle of Trafalgar.

Nelson's death provided the British government with the opportunity to treat Emma poorly, as if to erase the memory of her, a lower-class whore who had used her wiles to penetrate the highest echelons of English society and to snare its greatest man. They even banned her from her lover's funeral.

Nor did the government provide her with any support, as Nelson pleaded in his will. She was plagued by the hero's grasping relatives; his old shipmates tried to bribe her; men appeared from out of nowhere claiming they had "known" her back when she was Amy Lyon; creditors besieged her.

So harassed was Emma, that she voluntarily presented herself at a debtors' prison. In order to spare themselves from being locked in cells, people with the means could take accommodation within the three square mile area around the prison, known as the Rules. Within two months, friends had paid enough of her debt that Emma was allowed to leave, but she was soon publicly arrested and sent back to the Rules. Meanwhile, the love letters Nelson had written her—and which had been stolen by servants—were published. It was her reputation that suffered, not his, as if she was evil incarnate for having inflamed the passions of the unwitting hero.

One of her neighbours near Merton Place was able to sell enough of her possessions to pay Emma's bail. She hid out for a week with her daughter before taking a private boat to Calais in France.

She arrived with fifty pounds to her name, and her situation grew worse by the day. Emma died in Calais at age forty-nine of an abscessed liver.

The English continued to be titillated by her over the years as they simultaneously denigrated her.

In 1941, her memory was subjected to the humiliation of being portrayed as a ditzy airhead by a juiceless Vivien Leigh. The movie—*That Hamilton Woman*—begins with her as an old hag stealing a bottle of booze in Calais and telling her story to another inmate in jail. It ends when the tale is told.

Carolina Otéro
1868–1965

On a day in 1880, Carolina Otéro went over the convent wall in her home town in Spain and caught a train to Lisbon where she took a hotel room and rented a piano to accompany her singing. The man in the next room couldn't help but hear, and loved what he heard. He was the artistic director of the Avenida Theatre and he hired her immediately to sing and dance in the operetta *La Gran Via*. It wasn't long before she was the coddled mistress of a rich banker, but soon she grew bored and did a midnight flit. She arrived in Barcelona two days later, on her thirteenth birthday.

There Otéro appeared in another operetta and took up with a young man only a few years her elder. He gambled away her salary and she left for an engagement in Oporto, Portugal. Although chaperoned by the theatre manager and his wife, Otéro was kidnapped by the chief of police and taken to the home of the richest man in town, one Manuelo Domingo, and she became his mistress. When this liaison proved a disaster, Otéro was rescued by the elderly Count Tirenzo, but soon fell in love with an opera baritone named Guglielmo. They fought continually; the part of her earnings he didn't gamble away was the part she did. Otéro, in the words of a future biographer, had, by the time she was fifteen years old, been in jail for beating up a rival, and acquired three Andalusian grandees and an Italian husband "who was as handsome as Bizet's toreador."

IMAGE: Carolina "La Belle" Otéro by Jean Reutlinger, ca. 1902.

For the next forty years, Otéro's life would follow a similar pattern, but played out on a greater scale: terrific success, one extremely rich man after another, gambling, and incredible adventure. But it was all foreshadowed by her earliest days before the convent.

Otéro was born in 1868. Her mother, Carmencita, was a gypsy, and the model for the Carmen Virgin in the chapel at Cadiz. Otéro's father was a Greek soldier. While the father was gambling, the mother was dancing, singing, and telling fortunes. She also took lovers, one of whom shot and killed Otéro's father in a duel. When the girl was eleven years old, she was said to have the figure of a well-made seventeen-year-old.

Otéro hit Paris in 1889, at the age of eighteen, right in the middle of the glittering *belle époque*. She was soon the premier courtesan in that great time of *Les Grandes Horizontales*. What set her apart from her rivals was that she was a serious artist. After her Paris debut at the Cirque d'été, *Le Figaro* described her as "tall, dark and serpentine...skin burnt golden by the sun, eyes that flame, a mouth as appetizing as a pomegranate..."

She soon became the star of Les Folies Bèrgere.

The cartoonist Georges Goursat, known as SEM, after seeing her jump up on the table at Maxim's and launch into a sensual dance, wrote, "I feel that my thighs are blushing."

Otéro made a fortune performing in New York City, and what she didn't spend on gambling, she gave away. Back in Paris, she was taken care of by the Vicomte de Chênedollé, who spent his entire fortune on her. When the money ran out he killed himself. The Vicomte was but the first of seven to commit suicide on her account.

Otéro's next theatrical success was in Berlin at the Winter Garden. She was set up in a townhouse by yet another baron, who provided her with servants, horses, carriages, jewellery. Then it was on to Vienna where it was a prince, Edouard de Belime.

In Budapest, after a fandango, a nobleman addressed her, saying, "Mademoiselle, the most austere anchorite, living on vegetables and water, could not see you dance the fandango without throwing his sandals and vows to the devil."

In Moscow, at a private party she was presented naked on a silver platter. A newspaper reporter wrote that the scene was saved from vulgarity when her audience "went down on their knees...the strength and intensity that possessed these men before this perfection of lines proves that, whether the medium be the marble of the sculptor or the colours of the artist or living flesh-and-blood, man feels before Beauty the worshipfulness of Art."

In St. Petersburg, Otéro's first lover was the Grand Duke Peter, who wrote to her, "I have frequently imagined myself in love, but today it seems to me that I have never known before what love meant.... What joy to be able to give you everything you wish. What follies I would commit to please you..." He committed them, but it wasn't enough. She had clandestine meetings with Tsesarevich Nicholas, soon to be Nicholas II, the last tsar of Russia.

Rumour and legend surround the exploits of many females (and males) who lead outsized lives. Stories are passed around and often embellished in the retelling. But with Otéro, known by the time she was twenty-one as "La Belle Otéro," we not only have newspaper accounts, court records, and the diaries of her maid, but also the memoirs of others, many of them famous. For instance, when the writer who would come to be known as Colette was beginning her own stage career, she was befriended by Otéro and often invited to visit her on Sundays at one or another of her villas. Colette describes Otéro dancing for her own pleasure from ten in the evening until two in the morning. "She'd let her robe fly open... In the brown cleavage between two curiously shaped breasts like elongated fruit, firm and raised at the points, would sparkle carelessly a single diamond, a row of radiantly pink pearls or a bit of theatrical jewellery.... The sweat ran down to her thighs. She'd grab a sauce-stained napkin from the table and wipe her face, her neck, her armpits. Then she'd dance again and again."

Those "curiously shaped" breasts inspired the architect of the Hotel Carlton to model its two cupolas on them.

Otéro began an affair with Edward VII, Prince of Wales. She danced in his presence at clubs and cafés, and the future king would leave a napkin on his table with a clock face showing the time of their assignation. He bought her a hunting lodge outside of Paris, but she preferred the apartment on Champs-Élysées purchased for her by another Englishman. She was escaping from that man, an industrialist named Thompson, when she met a young man in the Bois de Boulogne and had sex with him in the open. Later, when Otéro refused to see him again, the young man threatened to kill himself, and did. Coming back from dinner that night she heard news vendors crying, "Belle Otéro Suicide."

Otéro next took up with the Duke of Westminster who invited her to spend his wealth, which one of his biographers described as "incalculable." Whenever they weren't together, Otéro might be seen with his friend, Kaiser Wilhelm II. He had her portrait painted, and she appeared as a gypsy beggar in a one-act play he wrote.

Students gave her parades in whichever city she appeared. One of the Vanderbilts offered Otéro his yacht. She had brief affairs with Italian poet Gabriele D'Annunzio and French statesman Aristide Briand. A jealous woman tried to kill her while Otéro was appearing in *Une Fête à Paris* in Seville, at the Théâtre Marigny. The shots missed, and once again she was a heroine in the press.

In June, 1912, at age fifty, Otéro debuted as the lead in *Carmen*. The reviews were extravagant. She was called a "sensuous, magnetic beauty," but "before all, a dramatic artist."

When World War I broke out, Otéro quit the stage to raise money and organize relief work. She also supported numerous orphans. The story is told of her purchasing from a sailor in the harbour at Nice a black boy in exchange for a bottle of cologne. She never denied the story.

After the war, La Belle Otéro thought it too late to return to show business. She felt she was no longer the ravishing beauty of only a few years before. When one looks at photographs of famous beauties and fabled courtesans, it is often difficult to fathom the power they held. Fashion changes, you think; or, They liked them chubbier then; or, She must have had some indefinable quality that the camera can't capture. Lola Montez, or Adah Menken, come to mind. But in the case of Otéro, it is all on display: unarguable beauty and a sensuous figure. In costume, her waist seems impossibly small, but photographs that show her with midriff exposed belie the notion of a corset. As a historian of the era put it, she was *"La belle des belles de la belle époque."*

Besides appearing in a couple of silent films, Otéro spent her time gambling, and over the years her considerable wealth vanished, her assets pledged to pay her debts. Besides money and jewellery, these assets included apartments and villas, as well as an island in the Pacific that had been given to her by the emperor of Japan.

In 1941, she moved into a suite of rooms at a hotel in the student quarter of Nice. A couple of years later, no longer able to afford the suite, Otéro took a single room in the same quarter. She lived on the proceeds of movie rights to her life story. A journalist visiting her in the early sixties noted that on her dresser was a photo of Maria Félix, who had played her in the film *La Belle Otero*. On one wall was the portrait commissioned by the kaiser. Above the counter that held her one-burner hot plate, was a plaque given to her in appreciation by the Republic of Argentina. She filled her time by playing the piano and guitar, and feeding pigeons from her balcony.

She died at age ninety-seven on April 11, 1965. The only people at the funeral service were a couple of neighbours, and three men in their forties—boys she had adopted years before. The croupiers from the casino in Juan les Pins sent an arrangement of flowers in the shape of a roulette wheel. It bore the inscription *"La Roue Tourne"* —"The Wheel Turns."

"I am the first in the East,
the first in the West,
and the greatest Philosopher
in the Western World;
Affirmed by me,
Timothy Dexter."

Engraved from the Life   by James Akin Newburyport.

The most Noble
Lord Timothy Dexter.

What a piece of work is Man!

how noble in reason! how infinite in faculties! in form & moving, how express & admirable!

Entered according to act of Congress June 1st 1805 by James Akin Newbury
AND SOLD BY THOMAS & WHIPPLE.

Timothy Dexter
1748–1806

There really was a man who shipped coal to Newcastle and, what's more, he made a fortune doing so.

Timothy Dexter, who referred to himself as the first Lord of America, was regarded as simple-minded, though funny and irascible. He had a head full of ideas, more energy than ten men, and loved to take a chance. Other, lesser, men, though of higher station in life, enjoyed presenting him the silliest business ideas they could think of.

When he sent bedpans to Barbados—after selling a ship's worth of mittens in Jamaica—they were accompanied by a note to his agent there, ordering the man to affix handles, after which the entire lot was bought and used as warming pans in the molasses industry. It was after this exploit that Dexter's betters in the town of Newburyport, Massachusetts, vexed by the upstart's luck, told him he should next send coal to Newcastle. Oblivious to the irony, Dexter filled an entire ship that arrived in England in the middle of a coal miners strike.

Back in the 1800s in America, society, particularly in New England, was rigidly structured. There were three class designations—upper, middle, and lower—and more significantly each of these was likewise so designated. People could only hope to rise one step within a main category. Dexter, who was born middle-lower, managed the

IMAGE: "Lord Timothy Dexter" engraving by James Akin, Courtesy of the American Antiquarian Society.

seemingly impossible by rising to middle-upper. Dexter himself was not surprised by his catapulting to near the top of the heap, for as he wrote of his birth, on January 22, 1747: "On this day in the morning A grat snow storme—the sines in the seventh house wives mars Came fored Joupeter stud by houlding the Candel—I was to be one grat man."

The great event occurred in nearby Malden, Massachusetts. At the age of eight, Timothy was indentured to a farmer for six and a half years. Then he apprenticed for three years in the leather trade. He learned to make britches and gloves, after which, dressed in his "freedom suit," he walked from Charlestown to Newburyport, where he opened a shop called The Sign of the Glove.

Everyone acknowledges that the man became almost indecently wealthy, but not even serious Dexter scholars address the problem of how he got his initial fortune. In 1769, at the age of twenty-two, Dexter was able to purchase his own store, and the next year to buy a boat. In 1770, he married a widow with two children and bought a house.

All this activity took an amount of money inconceivable to a young man recently indentured, or ever indentured. It calls to mind the line in the Ray Charles song: "them that's got are them that gets... How do ya get your first is still a mystery to me." The answer seems obvious, to this observer anyway: privateering. When trouble began brewing with the mother country, boats and ships from New England ports started preying on English ships. English captains had a habit of mistaking Newburyport for Boston. Dexter must have been lying in wait.

Prior to the American Revolution, the thirteen colonies were governed by the Continental Congress, which issued its own dollars, known as Continentals. For a time after the Revolution, the Continentals were valueless. Dexter, nevertheless, bought them at pennies on the dollar. Several years later, under Secretary of the Treasury Alexander Hamilton, the Continentals became exchangeable at par and, thus, Dexter made another fortune.

His ability to make money infuriated his betters but, even worse, his outrageous behaviour appeared to mock all they stood for.

He spent money wildly and continued to associate with the characters he knew when he was a lowly glove maker. Tramps were always welcome at his door; he took advice from astrologers and fortune tellers. He bought a large house and a real live lion to roam the grounds. He was to be seen in town trailed by what everyone thought was a pig, but which Dexter insisted was a dog. Besides this animal, he had an entourage of rascals, soothsayers, and your more interesting drunks.

When not walking, he went around town in a luxurious coach with a pair of cream-coloured horses, and would be driven past children skipping rope and chanting: "Dexter is a smart old man. Try and catch him if you can."

He bought his first ship while still in his thirties, and would eventually own three. Ship owners occupied the upper-upper class, but not ones who also owned lions and had necromancers to dinner and aired their private lives in print. Dexter often bought space in the local newspaper to tell the world the troubles he had with his shrewish wife. He was not criticized too much for this because everyone who ever met the woman came away agreeing with her husband.

His last big score came when he bought twenty-one thousand Bibles at twenty-one cents each. These he sent to the West Indies with a printed notice that every person should have one, or else he or she would probably go to hell. He advised purchasers it was necessary to kiss the Bible three times a day and pray to heaven. He sold them all at a dollar apiece.

What he did next must have alienated him even more from the good folks of the town: He quit trying to make money. "I found I had made money anuf; I hant speck alated sence..."

Dexter then bought an even larger house with larger grounds and commissioned a sculptor to produce seventy-six figures of men, women, and animals. These he put on pedestals. He had the three presidents of the republic on tall columns, but the positions of prominence were given to two columns featuring statues of Timothy Dexter: one at the east side of the grounds, which was festooned with a plague that announced "Number One in the East"; the other, on the opposite side of the grounds, announced "Number One in the West."

Of his statuary and outdoor oddities, including his tomb with a glass summer-house on top, he wrote: "I wants to make my Enemys grin in time Lik A Cat over A hot puding, and goue Away, and hang there heads Doun Like a Dogg bin After sheep."

So here he was, a filthy rich, loquacious nutcase who had given up making money, turned his home into a museum and, worse than all of this, had fellow oddballs and even Negroes over to sit on his French furniture. There was Black Luce, who eventually became his best friend, and Madame Hooper, his resident witch, famous for her double row of teeth. As well, Dexter had his own poet, Jonathan Plummer, who had been following Dexter around for years.

Dexter hired William Barley—a six-foot-seven strong man nicknamed "Dwarf Billey," the largest man in the country—to carry him around the property when his gout was acting up. Some days he was friendly to visitors, giving them fruit, plying them with strong drink, and often making passes at women of all ages. He walked around with a large pair of scissors and rewarded children with a lock of his hair. One day so many people came to call that he was practically bald by nightfall. Other days, he was not as congenial. He served a day in jail at Ipswich for shooting a fellow who persisted in asking stupid questions.

Although only semi-literate, Dexter, in his last years, produced a book that has been in print for nearly two hundred years, one of the classics of American literature: *A Pickle for the Knowing Ones; or Plain Truths in a Homespun Dress*. It probably started out as an explanation of his museum, but soon his pen got out of hand as it were, and roamed over such topics as the real nature of the devil, the habits of religious figures he had known, his marital difficulties, the planning of bridges and highways, and a complete description of the beating administered to him by a lawyer in nearby Chester when Dexter was caught spooning with the man's young lady friend.

As he wrote, "Nomatter what Dexter Rits, it Dus to make the Ladyes laf at the tea tabel."

And that it did.

But besides being a great work, *A Pickle* is the first modern work, as well as the first post-modern work. Knowing no boundaries of subject or genre, it also eschews punctuation. When readers complained about the lack of punctuation, Dexter brought out a second edition with a page at the end consisting of question marks, periods, commas, colons, semi-colons, and exclamation marks! He advised readers to use them to "peper and solt" the text as they pleased.

His last communication to the world appeared, as had so many others, in the local newspaper. A couple of weeks before he died, in 1806, he asked that learned men help with the matter that troubled him above all others, to wit: "Dus Angels hev wings?"

In the world of eccentrics and scalawags, Timothy Dexter was definitely beyond upper-upper.

Harry "The Hipster" Gibson 1915–1991

It was my good fortune to have known some of the last of the old breed of swinging jazz musicians. This was before jazz put on shorts and a ball cap and made nice. Many of these individuals are now legendary, as opposed to merely famous, and one of them seems more legendary than the rest.

Information about Harry Gibson is elusive; his activities are so strange that even conservative, just-the-facts jazz reference books feel compelled to mention them. According to *Jazz: The Rough Guide,* for instance, he conducted the female choir in a prison where he was serving time, wrote a hymn accepted by the Vatican for the Marian year, lived on an Indian reserve and married the chief's daughter, and more.

There was a Count, a Duke, and a King; a Bags, a Bird, and a Hawk; but no one knew what to call this cat, so he invented his own term: "hipster."

The kind of hipster he was is not to be confused with the hipster of today (some ironic dork who seems scared of his own shadow). He wasn't following a script; he wrote the script and then improvised on it. Before there was "hip" there was "hep," as in, "He's hep to the jive they're laying down." Jive talk was lingo particular to the world of jazz, but so many outsiders were coming on hep that it annoyed musicians. Musicians, therefore, replaced "hep" with "hip."

Photo of Harry Gibson, Diamond studio, New York, N.Y.(?), ca. Apr. 1947 by William P. Gottlieb.
Image courtesy of William P. Gottlieb Collection, Library of Congress.

And the first person known to have been called a "hipster" is Harry Gibson.

But he wasn't born a Gibson. He was born a Raab in 1915 to a musical family in the Bronx at the edge of Harlem. Harry was picking out tunes on the piano when he was three years old, and could play the current pop songs by the time he was five. One day, exploring the basement of the family music store, Harry chanced upon old music rolls from player pianos. He began to play along with the rolls, playing everything he heard, not realizing that many of the notes in each tune had been added on later. At thirteen he got with a band playing Saturday night dances at Starlight Park, which were broadcast on local radio. This led to a gig backing the singing waiters at a joint owned by the gangster Dutch Shultz. Harry moved on to an otherwise all-black band called the Chocolate Bars. When he wasn't playing, he hung around outside nightclubs in Harlem listening and learning. He got known as the crazy white kid who played like a grown-up black man. He began to pick up on black jive talk and add to it.

He was playing at the Rhythm Club, a sort of nightspot and union hall for black musicians, and doing take-offs on Fats Waller, telling people that he was the star pupil of the man himself. One night a large, jovial man started calling out requests and Harry played them—all Fats Waller tunes. The man stuffed a five-dollar bill in the kitty after every one. Patrons thought this real funny, but Harry didn't know why they were laughing. Finally the man said to Harry, "I just came around to hear what my star pupil sounds like."

Fats Waller hired him to be his intermission piano player at a club on 52nd Street, known as Swing Street for its proliferation of jazz spots. The job lasted until Fats left town a year later, after which Harry's style changed and he began to write songs. He played around the street for another five years backing musicians such as Billie Holiday, Charlie Parker, Coleman Hawkins, and Dizzy Gillespie. As well, he had a steady job with the more conservative Eddie Condon band, and became a fellow at the classically oriented Juilliard Graduate School.

During those days in the early forties, Harry, now Gibson, having taken his new surname from the label on a gin bottle, got together with another scalawag, Slim Gaillard, and invented a new song form called "vocalese," which is not, as often is the case, to be confused with scat singing. Scat singing substitutes non-verbal sounds for words, whereas vocalese uses syllables that make up ersatz words (for instance, Harry "The Hipster" Gibson's immortal phrase—coined fifteen years before Little Richard—"Wop bop a boodlee a webop, a wop mop bam"). Gaillard recorded his famous war resister song, "Flat Foot Floogie (with a Floy Floy)," and Gibson did the companion piece, "4F Ferdinand, the Frantic Freak."

Shortly thereafter Harry had his first big hit, "Boogie Woogie in Blue," and recorded it on a "Soundie." These were forties' music films played on Soundie machines and later on screens mounted atop jukeboxes. You can watch the documentary *Boogie in Blue* and other Hipster videos on YouTube, and if you do, what you will see is an uncanny forerunner of Jerry Lee Lewis: a cat with long blond hair combed back pumping the piano, standing up, fingers gone wild. The comparison to Jerry Lee is, however, primarily visual. Harry "The Hipster" was in another league as a piano player.

Harry was prone to giving his piano a beating, so he devised what he called a "breakaway" piano. He'd pound the thing, kick it, smash it, and at the end of a gig, it would fall completely apart, to be reassembled later.

In 1945, he was recruited to play at Billy Berg's Rendezvous club in Hollywood for $1,000 a week. He stayed a year. Berg asked him what this bebop was that he had been hearing about. Harry explained it and advised him to start booking acts like Dizzy Gillespie and Charlie Parker, which he did, and thus bebop came to the West Coast.

Harry had a couple of medium hits with "Handsome Harry, the Hipster" and "I Stay Brown All Year 'Round," which besides being a jive tune also commented on race relations. It got him in trouble in certain quarters. The controversy it caused—a white man singing about the situation of black men—was nothing compared to the fallout over his next song, the one that was his most popular but also, alas, led to his downfall: "Who Put the Benzedrine in Mrs. Murphy's Ovaltine?"

The number sold a ton of copies and got Harry plenty of jobs in clubs, at dances, on radio, and a part in a movie, *Junior Prom*, playing a guy who interrupts a music class and teaches the students about "the beat" so that pretty soon they're dancing between their desks. But the song also brought the heat down on him, primarily from the vice squad, and he was sued by Ovaltine. Club owners were reluctant to hire him for fear the cops would bust the joint.

He was rescued by Mae West who wanted him to play a hip sailor in her stage show *Come On Up (Ring Twice)*. The show toured for a year and, naturally, Mae and Harry became intimate.

After that, Harry still found work but not much of it. He played with Benny Carter and the Earl "Fatha" Hines band. One night at the Savoy Ballroom when Cab Calloway was playing, Harry walked onstage carry a large water-pipe filled with marijuana. He lit the pipe and handed it to Cab Calloway, who took a couple of deep tokes and jumped into his strutting, jiving act. Naturally the patrons loved it.

But the jobs were diminishing rapidly as rock and roll began to tighten its grip on the entertainment business. Ironically Harry, who could be said to have been playing rock and roll for years, couldn't cash in on it. Another person more or less put out of work by all this was the hip comedian Lord Buckley. The two hipsters had to open their own nightclub in Miami to get gigs, and their own record label to turn out recordings. It didn't last.

Harry perfected the disappearing acts he'd been doing for decades, materializing infrequently, playing piano in Akron, Ohio, or driving taxi in San Francisco. He was, in the language of the street, "scuffling." The sixties were a disaster for Harry and he left few traces. The seventies, however, with hippies everywhere, saw the re-emergence of Harry "The Hipster" Gibson, who had been dubbed a "hippie" by bandleader Stan Kenton thirty years earlier. He played in a band called the Rock Boogie Blues Jammers fronted by Mike Cochrane. Harry wrote charts for the band, but its members had no idea what they meant. When Harry appeared on stage he often tossed joints into the audience. Fearing busts, Cochrane convinced him to fill the papers with cigarette tobacco. Harry drank so much that Cochrane had to tell bartenders to water his drinks. Most of the time, Harry spoke black jive talk, which not even the 1970s hippies understood. Other times, he sounded like some Jewish gangster from a 1930s movie.

In 1989, at age seventy-four, Harry put out his most successful album ever. Although called *Who Put the Benzedrine in Mrs. Murphy's Ovaltine*, it was comprised of new songs, including one about his little grass shack in Hawaii made of "Maui Wowie," which could be smoked as well as lived in. There was also one about Shirley MacLaine and how cool she was.

Harry had always told people that if he got old and infirm, he'd kill himself rather than be a burden to others. The image of Harry "The Hipster" Gibson sitting in a wheelchair in an old folks home dribbling oatmeal down his chin and listening to piped-in soft rock favourites is impossible to fathom. In 1991, wasting away with a bad heart, he put a gun to his head and ended it all.

One of those musicians whom I was fortunate enough to hang around with for a time was another piano player, Joe Albany. I asked him about Harry. Joe replied: "He was crazy, man. Last I heard of him he had run away with some countess from Eastern Europe. Cat could play, though."

H.D. "Huge Deal" McIntosh 1876–1942

H.D. McIntosh. His nickname summed up the man perfectly: "Huge Deal." He made and lost fortunes time after time in his whirlwind of a life. Near the end of it, and not knowing he was near the end of it, the old rapscallion (who had promoted boxing matches, and owned newspapers, theatres, and auditoriums) fell on hard times, but got back in the game by opening a chain of milk bars in London. "His comeback was inevitable," declared a magazine back home in Australia. "If he had not opened milk bars, he would probably have made a fortune selling moustache cups to ballerinas or promoting an all-in wrestle between Hitler and the Archbishop of Canterbury."

A rough, tough customer, he had a heart of gold. He was a "two-fisted mystery," said an actress from one of his Tivoli shows.

Hugh Donald McIntosh was born in Sydney in 1876. At age seven, Hughie, as he was called, asked his busy mother if he might go to faraway Adelaide with a grown-up man he knew. Her answer was a distracted "Yes."

The man was a tinker, and he and the future Huge Deal went "Waltzing Matilda." When they reached Broken Hill, Hughie got a job at one of the mines separating ore from quartz. He held that job for a year and a half when, not yet nine years old, he again went on the tramp. A detractor later called him a liar, insisting that when Hughie left his Sydney home he wasn't seven years old, he was nine.

Image courtesy of the Australian Variety Theatre Archive.

Hughie spent three years bumming around doing any job he could find. Back in Sydney, at age twelve, he got work as an assistant to a doctor. His spare time was passed in a gym run by Larry Foley, an ex-fighter known as "the man who taught Australia to fight," who taught Hughie to fight.

The doctor died when Hughie was sixteen, so once more he went roaming, working at dozens of jobs. In 1893, he appeared on stage in Melbourne as a chorus boy in *Sinbad the Sailor*. But his first financial success occurred in Sydney where he proved to be a champion seller of meat pies, working the race courses, boxing matches, beaches, and brothels. After his marriage in 1897 to Marion "May" Backhouse, a painting teacher, McIntosh took a job with a catering company as a bouncer. Two years later, he was running the business. As well, he opened the Physical Culture Hall, and promoted his first professional boxing match in 1900. He was twenty-four years old. Next, he got into bicycle racing, which had an immense following. He promoted races on a large scale and, after one event, discovering that the riders had fixed the race, stormed into the locker room and, in the words of a reporter, "laid out the guilty riders one at a time."

The next year, he ran for city council. He lost and was taken to court by the winner. Charged with slander, McIntosh denied calling his opponent a thief, but admitted to calling him "a dirty, scurrilous, unmanly cur." And he added, "I still feel that way."

Next, McIntosh ran a chain of guesthouses in the Blue Mountains of New South Wales, but when the US "Great White Fleet"— comprised of sixteen thousand men—arrived, he knew his first fortune had come with them. He leased every available dancehall, restaurant, and theatre in Sydney. Then he got the idea for a fight —a heavyweight world championship bout. McIntosh matched World Champion Tommy Burns with Australian Bill Squires. Toward this end McIntosh, dressed like a bum, approached the owner of some leasable land at Rushcutters Bay and got the rights for two pounds a week, with an option to buy. In six weeks he built what was then the largest arena in the world.

When the sailors hit the beach, they ate at his restaurants, drank at his pubs, attended organized dances at McIntosh's halls, and watched the Burns-Squires fight in his new Sydney arena.

In three weeks and two days, McIntosh had built another stadium in Melbourne, where Burns knocked out Clubber Lang in six rounds.

McIntosh's next fight promotion was not only his grandest, but is recognized by many boxing historians as being the most significant contest of all time. McIntosh was able to match Burns, a white Canadian, with the black American Jack Johnson, a.k.a. the "Galveston Giant." It was the first time a black man had ever been permitted to challenge for the heavyweight championship, then regarded as the ultimate symbol of manhood. To get Burns in the ring, McIntosh offered him £6,000, twice the highest amount of money ever paid a fighter. Later, when asked why he had paid Burns so much, McIntosh made a remark that lives on in the vocabulary: "You got to spend money to make money."

Hugh Donald McIntosh discovered his nickname one afternoon on the train between Melbourne and Sydney when he heard two drunks talking about the upcoming fight. "Who," one drunk asked his partner, misreading the promoter's name, "is this Huge Deal McIntosh?"

The crowd that turned up for the Burns-Johnson fight in Sydney on Boxing Day, 1908, was not only the largest ever to see a boxing match anywhere in the world, it was the largest group of people ever assembled for anything in Australian history. A few minutes before the bell for the first round, Johnson—who had only been promised £1,000 to get in the ring—challenged McIntosh, demanding more money or he would't fight. Huge Deal reached into his jacket pocket and came up with a revolver, which he pointed at Johnson's head. "If you're not in the ring in two minutes," he said, "I'll blow your brains all over the floor." Johnson entered the ring, and McIntosh refereed the fight. The cops stopped the bout in the fourteenth round, and as soon as word of the result went out over the wire, riots began. The new heavyweight champion of the world was a black man.

McIntosh took the two fighters on a circuit of vaudeville theatres, where they sparred with others and talked about the fight. He made a small fortune. Then he went around the world with the fight film. He made a larger fortune. When he reached New York, he was met at the dock by John L. Sullivan—a.k.a. the Boston Strong Boy, the first heavyweight champion of gloved boxing—and the old gunslinger "Bat" Masterson.

Back home in Sydney, McIntosh expanded his promotions to include a Wild Australia show, carnivals, concerts, and eventually theatres. In 1912, he sold his Sydney stadium and gained control of the Tivoli theatre chain. The takeover was big news, prompting *Punch* to call him "the personification of the hustler" and "the kind of man who might have captained a pirate ship."

McIntosh brought in all sorts of acts for his theatres, from ragtime piano players to playlets by George Bernard Shaw, and he employed future stars like W.C. Fields. In London to scout entertainers, he was asked to vacate his suite at the Savoy because he had covered the walls with Tivoli posters. McIntosh concocted a scheme: He sent a letter to the king merely discussing the funding of British sports. Before he could pack to leave, a letter came for him bearing the return address of Buckingham Palace; it was simply a polite acknowledgement of the receipt of his original letter, but the staff at the hotel were none the wiser. Suddenly McIntosh was a favoured guest of the Savoy.

McIntosh was unstoppable—at least for another decade and a half. He bought several news and sporting papers in 1916; invented the Tango Tea craze—patrons would sip tea while scantily clad dancers performed; tried to organize McIntosh's Rough Riders during WWI; staged serious plays; promoted concerts; travelled the world (usually with at least one female companion who was not his wife); leased a manor house with 243 hectares near Canterbury from the heirs of Lord Kitchener, the hero of Khartoum; and generally continued making vast sums of money. Huge Deal was also a huge womanizer. One of his stage managers declared, "He'd go through anything with long hair on it."

McIntosh associated with all manner of people from all strata of society. Some of these tended to be rough customers. He kept a piece of sheet music on his desk rolled to conceal a lead pipe, which he was not adverse to using. Artist Norman Lindsay remembers that the tune that wrapped the pipe was a lullaby titled, "Sing Me to Sleep, Mother."

McIntosh gave money to hospitals and charities; organized the installation of the cenotaph at Martin Place in downtown Sydney; hosted innumerable parties and receptions; and socialized with Sir Arthur Conan Doyle, H.G. Wells, Rudolph Valentino, and Charlie Chaplin. Then two things happened: talkies, and the worldwide stock market crash.

First, he sold *The Sunday Times*. A rival paper declared, "He had tried to turn the paper into a reflection of the Barnum circus that was his own life." His other papers soon followed; then the interests that leased his theatres went bankrupt. He fled to his estate in England, and turned a corner of his property into a model farm and raised angora rabbits. Nobody would come to the new plays he produced in England because movie tickets were a quarter of the price. By 1932, he was bankrupt. He sold his grand home in Australia, and moved into a four-pounds-four-shillings-a-week cottage in Sydney with his wife.

But this was far from the end of Huge Deal. Soon he was once again successful as the operator of the Tivoli Sponge Bakery, making sponge cakes. Success, however, ruined the business because it attracted many imitators with more capital.

McIntosh got back into boxing and made some money, but not enough to begin to pay his creditors. Next he took a job for a year managing Bon Accord, a guest house in the Blue Mountains. When the year was out, in 1934, he left Australia for the last time, travelling third-class with his wife to England. Within a few months, he had picked himself up yet again and was running a successful milk bar on London's Fleet Street. Soon there was a second, a third, and eventually twenty Black and White Milk Bars throughout the country. But, as with the Tivoli Sponge Bakery, competition laid him low.

He went back to promoting bicycle racing, and sold a series of reminiscences to Australian papers under the title "Champagne Days of a Fighting Millionaire."

McIntosh entered the timber business just as war was declared in 1939. The next year, he was portrayed as a social-climbing hustler who owned a boxing stadium in the Australian film *Come Up Smiling*. The year after that, he was diagnosed with colon cancer and died in London on February 2, 1942, at the age of sixty-five. At the end, he had only two pounds to his name. Friends paid for his cremation.

A lot of men fancy themselves hustlers and entrepreneurs, pulling off vast projects by brains or energy or chicanery, but in comparison they are only little deals. There has only been one "Huge Deal."

Victor Lustig
1890–1947

In the early 1920s, a dude in spats and a Saville Row suit, calling himself Count Victor Lustig, paid a call to the bank in a mid-sized Kansas town and announced he wished to buy a notoriously worthless farm that had been on the market for a decade. He offered ten times what the farm was worth. The bankers were so overcome by greed, and so befuddled by Lustig's smooth line of talk, that the con man left town two days later with $25,000.

This type of incident, repeated dozens of times in Lustig's career, is not what makes Lustig the most audacious con man in known history.

IMAGE: "Count" Victor Lustig (notorious counterfeiter), 1937; Bettmann/CORBIS, used under license.

He may have been the greatest, too, but that is open for debate. Some would maintain the honour has to go to Joseph "Yellow Kid" Weil, but the Kid never sold the Eiffel Tower. Lustig did—twice.

Lustig made little effort to cover his tracks, and was apprehended for the Kansas bank caper a few weeks later when the cops burst into his hotel room in New York. They were accompanied by a sheriff and a lawyer to take the ersatz count back to Kansas. On the train, Lustig told the lawyer that the worst possible thing for the town would be to have him stand trial. The bankers' lives would be ruined and there'd be a run on the bank; no one would want their money kept in an establishment so easily swindled. By the time they reached Chicago, not only had Lustig convinced the lawyer to let him go in order to avoid scandal, but had persuaded the man that he, the Count, should be reimbursed to the tune of $1,000. When the lawyer started to go apoplectic, Lustig shrugged and said, "Okay, let's go to trial." A few minutes later, the Count was on his way back to New York with a thousand bucks in his pocket.

And *that* kind of manoeuvre is what makes him the most audacious con man in history.

He was born in a small town in Austria-Hungary (now the Czech Republic) in 1890, his family respectable and middle-class. After boarding school in Germany, Lustig went to Paris where he became skilful at bridge, poker, billiards, and women. A knife fight over one of the latter left him with a wide scar that extended from the corner of his left eye to the lobe of his left ear.

Lustig made his way by hustling pool and cards, and by 1911 was working the transatlantic ships. During these voyages he became apprenticed to a lanky, six-and-a-half-foot-tall shark called Nicky Arnstein, who taught him the value of patience when working a mark. Arnstein was a compatriot of Arnold "The Brain" Rothstein—a kingpin of the Jewish mob in New York—and was married to Broadway star Fanny Brice. When World War I put an end to the transatlantic trade, Arnstein introduced Lustig to the big-time underworld. Arnstein went to jail for a major swindle involving Liberty Bonds. The police recovered most of the bonds, but not the $25,000 worth that Lustig would use for years as a prop.

In Montreal and Pittsburgh, Lustig set up wire stores and came away with fortunes. A wire store is an elaborate con based on convincing a greedy mark that you are able to get the results of horse races before they are officially announced because you have a close contact at the telegraph office—hence, the "wire." This big con is very much like a stage play, and the con man is the director. It requires different sets and actors playing their parts. Anyone who has watched the movie *The Sting* has seen how the wire store works.

After putting over wire stores, Lustig went to Florida where there was a land boom in progress. The Sunshine State at the time was a magnet for the nouveau riche and strivers and, thus, also attracted con men and hustlers. But Lustig wasn't interested in selling underwater lots; he had something better: a money-printing machine. In fact, he had several money machines. They were well crafted, made of mahogany, about a foot square and three inches high, with narrow slots at two ends and elaborate dials on the other two sides.

In Florida, Count Lustig finessed his first mark for a week before mentioning the box. The mark was perfect; he'd started out as a mechanic and made lots of money during the war from government contracts for engine parts. He was insecure, however, over his failure to be accepted by the old-money crowd. As well, his fortunes were declining with the war being over. Lustig let him know that he had a machine that would duplicate one-dollar, five-dollar, hundred-dollar bills, what have you, each with a different serial number. When the mark expressed his excitement, Lustig said, "As a matter of fact, I was going to run off a $1,000 bill this afternoon. Do you want to watch?"

Lustig inserted a $1,000 bill into the box, along with a piece of blank paper cut to the size of the bill, and the mark nodded when the count stressed that the process would take six hours, time enough for the special chemical bath to take effect.

Six hours later, Lustig carefully pressed buttons and adjusted knobs, and from the slots emerged two damp $1,000 bills. The count urged the mark to take the bills to a bank and have them checked for authenticity. They were, of course, real.

The man returned to the count's hotel and offered $25,000 for the machine. The count shrugged. "Why should I sell it when I can just make my own $25,000?"

Lustig eventually allowed himself to be persuaded. He took the money and left the hotel, reminding the mark that it was necessary to wait six hours for the process to be completed successfully.

It turned out, Lustig didn't have to make a run for it. As the story goes, when the machine refused to duplicate his money, the mark assumed it was his own fault. He went on trying to operate the box for years and never went after the count.

The money-printing machine, also known in the trade as the Romanian box, was never more than a sideline for Lustig. But it once proved his means of getting out of jail. Lustig had been busted in Oklahoma and was waiting to stand trial for swindling the richest man in town. The sheriff was an uncouth man full of braggadocio, and Lustig played him, eventually selling the box for $10,000 and his freedom.

After swindling $50,000 out of an Illinois tractor salesman who wanted to be a Broadway producer, Lustig repaired to Paris and was languishing at an outdoor café when he decided to sell the Eiffel Tower. Right there in the papers was a story about the city being strapped for funds. Someone was quoted as saying they ought to tear down the hideous tower and sell it for scrap. Lustig enlisted the aid of a partner (a Franco-American con man named Robert Arthur Tourbillon), gathered forged government stationery, rented a room at the Hôtel de Crillon, and wrote letters to five scrap-iron dealers, inviting them to a confidential meeting where, posing as a city works chief, he disclosed that the Eiffel Tower was for sale. After thoroughly checking out the five men, Lustig contacted his choice, Andre Poisson, and told him the Eiffel Tower was his. Not only did Lustig get the money for the tower, he also got a kickback from the scrap-iron dealer for arranging the deal.

A couple of weeks later, Lustig was in Chicago putting one over on none other than Al Capone. Lustig had some organized crime connections, having worked with Arnstein, Rothstein, Legs Diamond, and Capone's former boss, Johnny Torrio. So Capone was able to check him out. Lustig told Capone that he could turn the crime boss's $50,000 into half a million in two months. Capone went for it. Lustig was not dumb enough to abscond with the money; he returned two months later with the untouched bills still in Capone's envelope. He handed them over to the crime boss, apologizing, admitting that he was not able to make the connections that were necessary. When he got up to go, Capone, feeling sorry for him, gave him $5,000 from the envelope—which was what Lustig had been hoping for all along.

Back in Paris, having attempted to sell the Eiffel Tower a second time to another group of scrap dealers, Lustig was arrested by French police and handed over to American officials on an extradition order —brought about by the disgruntled Illinois tractor salesman. Lustig was put on board a ship bound for New York. The count knew the authorities would be waiting at customs to bring him to Illinois. Two days out from New York, the count cabled the Secret Service, saying he had information for them about a major counterfeiting ring in the United States. Thus, when the ship docked, he was met by both Illinois and federal authorities. The Feds prevailed, of course, and held the count in custody for three days, finally letting him go on the basis of his bogus information, which they believed.

Lustig might have continued in the usual manner except he abandoned the con man's code and got mixed up in a counterfeiting scheme. Not surprisingly, the counterfeit money was the best work ever seen in America. Tom Shaw, the man who had engraved the plates, ratted out Lustig. The police were amazed because they'd been looking to pin something on Lustig for years. He was sent to the Federal House of Detention in New York City, which the government had proudly proclaimed to be escape proof. Lustig escaped the day before his trial.

Several weeks later, he was apprehended again in Pittsburgh. On his person were letters of credit issued under several different names, and a gold key to a safe deposit box that held twenty-three passports. Lustig begged the cops to let him go because he had something in the works with the owner of a Canadian hockey team. "Just half an hour with the man, gentlemen, and I will be $50,000 richer. I'll share it with you."

The cops didn't buy it, but they did go and tell the hockey club owner that the man he had planned to meet was a crook. The man refused to believe them, and tried to get Lustig out of jail.

The count was convicted of fraud and counterfeiting after pleading guilty. He was sentenced to twenty years in Alcatraz. It was his forty-ninth arrest in the United States and his first conviction. He died in prison of pneumonia in March, 1947, at age fifty-seven. The death certificate listed his occupation as "Apprentice Salesman."

Honoré Jaxon
1861–1952

Had you been strolling down 34th Street in Manhattan back on December 12, 1951, maybe as a tourist headed for the Empire State Building just down the way, you would have come upon a most curious sight: a massive collection of books and papers commandeering the sidewalk for eleven metres, stacked two metres high and three metres deep. Perched on this mountain of bundles and crates was a little ninety-year-old man with a white beard, threadbare black suit, black cowboy hat, and two-tone wingtip shoes. Passersby heard him speaking in an incongruous, booming voice about injustice—done to him, to the Indians, and to the workers of the world.

IMAGE: Honoré Joseph Jaxon with tons of books and magazines.
(Photo by Hal Mathewson/NY Daily News Archive via Getty Images). Used under license.

A cop on the beat was heard to remark, "Hey, this is New York. We're used to characters, but this one...!"

The fellow sat out there all day and slept there all night. Having been evicted from his apartment, he had nowhere else to go, and he had to protect his "archive"—a huge collection of, among other things, Métis-related literature, which he hoped would be used to establish a museum in their honour. The next morning when he emerged from his cave dug between stacks of papers, he was the talk of the town. The old man was described by the *New York Daily News* as "Major Henri Jaxon, son of an Indian maiden and an adventurous Virginia trapper...born in the sweet grass hills of Montana...and once tried for treason by the Canadian government."

Well, that's who and what he was in his heart and in his mind, since over the previous decade or so of his life his mind had roamed completely free over imaginary prairies and plains. Of course, his mind had been unfettered for a lot longer than that. The "treason" part, however, was true.

When he was born on May 13, 1861, the name on his birth certificate was William Henry Jackson, but to point this out seems, in light of his incredible journey through life, somehow another injustice.

It was in Toronto, born to strict Methodist parents recently arrived from England, where he first saw the light of day. He was inadvertently saved from a life of dour righteousness by a father who was interested in politics, and was a failure in business. When his son was nine years old, the father let him read a newspaper article about a "half-breed" out in the Territories who was stirring up trouble, a man named Louis Riel. The boy had a contrary opinion to that expressed by the newspaper; he was sympathetic to Riel and his followers. The father took Willie, as he was known, to a political meeting. His mother wrote to her sister in England that the boy returned that evening "terribly excited." Right there are the main themes of his life: the Métis, injustice, politics, and being "terribly excited."

When the rest of the family moved west, the boy stayed behind to study classics at the University of Toronto. He did well in school, becoming fluent in Greek and Latin, but had to withdraw a couple of days before obtaining his degree because his father's bankruptcy made it impossible for him to continue. In 1882, Jackson travelled west to join his family in Prince Albert, Saskatchewan (then part of the Northwest Territories). The last train stop was Qu'Appelle, nearly five hundred kilometres from his folks in Prince Albert. But that didn't bother the boy; he walked the rest of the way.

Jackson turned his hand to various jobs, all without success. In 1884, when word spread that Riel was returning from exile, he was there to meet him. The two men became fast friends and soon Jackson was Riel's secretary. In his journal, Riel asked Jesus to "take care of ...William Henry Jackson...[my] special friend."

Though Jackson's father dreamed of converting the Métis to Protestantism, his son converted to Catholicism. On March 18, 1885, Jackson was baptized and given the name "Honoré Joseph Jaxon." Riel stood as his godfather.

According to intelligence reports of the North West Mounted Police, "Jaxon seems to be a right hand man of Riel...I believe he does more harm than any Breed among them." When fighting broke out, Jaxon was arrested by the NWMP and shipped to Regina in a wagon while chained to an old Indian man. At night he was staked out on the ground.

Jaxon was charged with "treason-felony" (the "felony" meant that if found guilty, he would not be executed). He wanted a trial so he could speak about injustice to the Métis, the Indian, and the settler. He was denied this right because the case had already been decided in private by the Crown, the defence attorney, and Jaxon's family. He was to be declared insane and sent to a lunatic asylum in Lower Fort Garry, near Winnipeg. The hearing took little more than an hour.

Jaxon was in the asylum only six weeks before escaping. Others had gotten away from the place, but had all been recaptured. Jaxon was the first to avoid apprehension. Five days later, he crossed the border into Minnesota. After Riel was executed, Jaxon began hitting the lecture circuit through the Midwest. Following a speech in Chicago organized by anarchists, a newspaper described him as obviously a Métis with "his dark complexion and high cheek bones."

Soon Jaxon was famous as an anarchist speaker. *The Chicago Tribune* stated he was "little less than a demigod" to "the ignorant class he gathered around him."

He worked construction to make a living, but gave most of his money away—although there couldn't have been many who needed it more—and got involved sponsoring a model commune at Topolabampo Bay in Mexico.

By 1890, he was living in a room in Chicago done up to resemble a Métis hunter's shack and calling himself Honoré Jaxon, and so he would remain, except for the honorific of major, which he bestowed upon himself a decade later.

He was loved by workers and bohemians, by anarchists and slumming society figures. When the *Tribune* called him "an Indian for revenue," he decided to take revenge. He organized the World Conference of Anarchists, and to host the event rented a room in the *Tribune* building next door to the publisher's office—something rival newspapers appreciated.

All the publicity was hurting the construction business he'd set up, so Jaxon got out of town for a while after being hired by a mining company to explore some properties in Ontario. He returned in time to speak for Indian rights at the opening of the Chicago World's Fair in 1893.

Next, in 1894, Jaxon joined Coxey's Army, that great group of men and women that marched to Washington to promote public works projects for the unemployed. Jaxon, dressed as a Métis, and carrying a blanket and a hatchet, led the Chicago contingent.

Then he joined the Baha'i faith and fell in love with Aimée Montfort, a young French-Canadian schoolteacher, whom he married in 1898. He even made an attempt at being conventional, which to him meant designing a tunnelling machine and patenting a device to protect buildings during earthquakes. Soon it became clear that even a conservative Jaxon was too much for his wife, who had the audacity to insist they spend money on running water and electric light. They decided to live separately.

Jaxon spent two years in a wagon—a "prairie schooner"—travelling to visit all the old sites in Saskatchewan.

A reporter for *The Saturday Evening Post* caught up with him in 1907: "He looks like an Indian, talks like a graduate of Oxford, writes like a professor of rhetoric and he lives in two cluttered rooms in back of a pickle factory."

Jaxon ran for office as the federal representative for Prince Albert, and when he lost, went to England on a speaking tour. More years were spent speaking throughout the US and Canada, and he got involved with helping anarchist revolutionaries in Mexico. Arriving in New York City to give a speech in 1919, he decided to stay.

When Aimée received some money from her family, she sent some of it to Jaxon who bought a few properties in the Bronx. On one of these, Jaxon started in 1923 to erect what he called his "Fort." His building material consisted of seven hundred large ammunition cases obtained (legally) from the US Army. This edifice —eight metres high, not counting the tall, tin cupola—became famous as the Box Castle Garden.

In 1927, a fire destroyed his castle and many of his books and papers. He claimed the mobster Dutch Schultz was behind the fire. Jaxon moved to another property and, calling himself Buffalo Heart, started building Camp Contentment. Desperately poor by now, he acceded to his wife's wishes to sell one or more of his properties, but no sooner did he put the places on the market than the Depression hit. The city stepped in to expropriate his land, but Jaxon protested, saying they didn't have the right because he was an Indian and the Indians had never signed their land away. His old friend Frank Lloyd Wright visited him in 1936, and told reporters back in Chicago that Jaxon was "living in a big barn amid vast piles of newspapers, dreaming world reform while rats raced past him."

In 1942, his wife died and the city demolished his latest fort. He was eighty years old and homeless, yet he could write to his sister: "I am now free for new and joyous adventures."

His associates in his last decade included the Chanlers—a patrician New York family—and a Nazi sympathizer named Karl

Mertig. Jaxon had fallen in with the latter because Mertig, as a Nazi, protested the treatment of native peoples by the American government. The Chanlers and Mertig each provided the old man with at least one meal a week.

Despite his age, Jaxon worked three jobs: rising at five in the morning to stoke the furnace of his apartment building; running a newsstand on 82rd Street; and collecting garbage from a building on 85th Street. In the summer of 1951, he was run over by a car, but let the driver move on because he knew it was not the man's fault.

One day a friend known as Wall Street Abe took him to the offices of *Bowery News* where he was roundly welcomed. It was the editor of the paper, Harry Baronian, who later rescued Jaxon from his perch atop the massive sprawl of papers after he was evicted from his apartment. Baronian, an ex-hobo, had a truck bring along sixty of Jaxon's boxes. The rest were sold for scrap. At the paper's offices, the Old Majah, as Jaxon was known, was washed and kept fed by an ex-snake charmer called Boxcar Betty. Additional assistance was supplied by Barnonian and Bozo Clarke, a clown known as the "Crown Prince of the Hoboes."

But William Henry Jackson, a.k.a. Honoré Jaxon, had undergone too much hardship: hit by a car, sleeping on the street, eating hardly anything. He suffered a serious relapse and was taken by his Bowery friends to Bellevue Hospital. On his deathbed, he told Baronian he had to get well in order to take all his books and papers back to Saskatchewan to build a library for native peoples. Jaxon died on January 10, 1952.

George Manolesco
1871–1911

He is the model for all the charming scoundrels of modern history.
Two dozen movies were based on his exploits. He was played in silents
by Conrad Veidt and the great Ivan Mozzhukhin, and in talkies,
most notably, by Herbert Marshall in Ernst Lubitsch's *Trouble in
Paradise*, considered by many critics to be the best romantic comedy
ever made. In literature he is Raffles, Arsène Lupin, and Felix Krull.
But the real man is even less familiar than H.H. Lahovary, the Duke
of Otranto, George Mercandente, or Gaston Monescu, all of which
were his pseudonyms. Born Georgin Manulescu, he was a Romanian known to the newspapers of his time as George Manolesco,
"King of Swindlers" and "Prince of Thieves."

IMAGE: George Manolesco, "Prince of Thieves" 1889.

In a game of cards, when he laid out his hand and raked in the pot, you'd see the ace you thought was hidden up your sleeve. After arriving penniless in Paris one dawn in a boxcar filled with goats, he was driven to dinner that evening in his own coach-and-four. His life was one of nearly non-stop adventure. It's all in police records. He really was, in his own unique way, a genius.

Born in Ploieşti in Romania in 1871, he never knew his mother, and his father was an unhappy and unsuccessful army officer whom young George often had to escort home after he'd gotten drunk and lost all his money playing cards. But the boy liked to watch the men gamble, and he was befriended by a soldier who had been a stage magician until losing a couple of fingers in a brawl. The man taught him sleight of hand and card-sharping tricks, and soon George was winning his pals' money. The friends began to steal valuables from their parents in their eagerness to play, and when they got in trouble, said George had stolen the things. The police were called and George's father forced him to enlist in the service. He was fourteen. He soon ran away from the brutality he witnessed, but was apprehended in the Ottoman Empire (now Turkey) and imprisoned for a month. Within the year he had deserted again, eventually washing up in Constantinople, a stowaway on an Ottoman tramp.

Manolesco survived at first by sleeping in the bazaar and eating at missions. He spent his days on the *Grand Rive* looking for opportunity. He found it when the poodle of a rich woman dashed into traffic out front of the Bristol Hotel. Manolesco darted into the street and rescued the animal. The women, a countess, invited him back to her suite to meet her husband, who was attached to the French embassy. The boy told such a dazzling story of his young life that the couple gave him a job at their villa. Soon he began an affair with the countess, which lasted for three months until she wanted to lend him to another countess. He took umbrage and departed with six boxes of diamonds.

In Athens, Manolesco took up with a Hungarian cabaret singer who assisted him in spending the money he had gotten for the jewels. She ran out when the money did, and a desperate Manolesco sought help from the Romanian consul. When he was refused, Manolesco went to the man's hotel suite with a pistol and shot himself. At the hospital, he was the talk of the staff because he survived the bullet wound. The ward was visited by Queen Olga of Greece, the daughter of a Russian grand duke. The queen took a liking to Manolesco, got him a private room, and visited frequently. She had a carriage waiting when he left the hospital, gave him money, and spent several days touring the sights of Greece with him. Manolesco was always discreet about their relationship.

The queen gave him a ticket to Romania, but at the port of Piraeus he exchanged it for one to Marseille, where he was soon penniless and living on the beach of the Old Port, existing by selling dirty postcards. Manolesco made his way to Paris and began calling at jewellery stores, using sleight-of-hand tricks learned back in Ploieşti to steal diamonds. Newspapers claimed "a crew of professional thieves is responsible for these robberies."

Soon Manolesco was crashing society events at private homes, casing them, and returning to pull jobs, often gaining entry by climbing the sides of the building or clambering over rooftops. At one party he met the duchess of Trevolle, a notorious libertine, and became her lover, with her husband's permission, but much to the chagrin of her friend, the painter Toulouse-Lautrec. She knew of Manolesco's occupation, but made him desist while they were together. The affair began to dissolve after a snide remark by Lautrec.

After a couple more years of this up-and-down existence, from the high life to the low life and back again, Manolesco was busted in Vienna and sent to prison for two years of hard labour. On his release, he took a ship bound for Canada and while on board won $5,000 playing cards. He didn't like the look of Halifax, and continued on to Chicago, where he turned into the Duke of Otranto. On the train going west, he won money gambling and stole pearls, some of them from a rich widow. At his hotel in San Francisco he was confronted by a fellow passenger with a captain of detectives in tow. This man was not a victim of Manolesco's capers, but claimed to be doing his duty as an upright citizen. Manolesco pleaded innocence and was told to report to the station house the next morning at nine o'clock. In little more than twelve hours, in a town he didn't know, but with the help of a bent private eye, Manolesco managed to sell the pearls and have them sent to the insurance company, which presented them to the rich widow the next morning before his appointment with the police. The widow was so grateful that she and Manolesco spent the next two days together. On the morning of the third day, Manolesco left her room and caught a ship for Hawaii. Again, he had her pearls with him.

Thomas Mann, at the end of his life, wrote a novel completely unlike the rest of his work. It concerned the adventures of a daring thief and con man. Mann had read about Manolesco. The eponymous protagonist was Felix Krull, named after the "upright citizen" who had summoned the cops on Manolesco.

On and on it went, a dizzying parade of scandal and skulduggery. One evening in Nice, after an evening with a woman who retired to her room with fewer jewels than she had when they went to dinner, Manolesco returned to his room and fell asleep in a chair. He woke as a thief entered his room through a window. Manolesco studied the man, and only as the thief was leaving did he stop him. The man was a Corsican named Pellicio, and the two became great friends. Manolesco hired the man as a valet, but Pellicio's real job was to keep an eye out for opportunities. They made a great pair for ten years.

Manolesco saved the funds of an old lady in Zurich and came to the aid of the king of Albania, who presented him with a document bestowing the title Baron d'Argente Viva (Baron of Quick Money). Manolesco tried marriage, but couldn't last more than six weeks. By 1902, he was so notorious that his movement was severely restricted. Forced to act out of desperation, he was arrested in Baden-Baden for a job in Lucerne, and pleaded insanity to avoid another stretch in prison. He was judged not guilty, but sentenced to an asylum for life. Within six weeks, he had escaped.

The story of his moonlight flit caused a worldwide sensation. On the advice of his lawyer, Manolesco gave himself up to police in Vienna. They could not extradite him or charge him with any crime because he had been judged not guilty by the Swiss court.

Returning to his old ways was impossible so, down on his luck, Manolesco accepted an offer to return to Romania and write his life story for the newspapers (his memoirs would become bestsellers in Germany in 1905). Manolesco was greeted as a hero wherever he went.

When the money ran out, Manolesco managed to get to New York where he met a Hungarian sideshow owner who hired him to go to the St. Louis World's Fair in 1904 and manage "Feher's East European Midget Show." When Feher realized his employee was George Manolesco, he tried to capitalize on the fact, the result being that the "Prince of Thieves" skipped out, along with a showgirl from Quebec City.

After months wandering through Canada, Manolesco wound up in the unlikely town of Alonsa, Manitoba, that happened to be filled with miners returned from the Yukon and Nome gold rushes. He set up as a gambler, and did all right until he fell on the ice and his shattered right arm was set by a drunken doctor. When it became infected, Manolesco went to Montreal where another doctor had to break the arm and set it again. In 1906, back in Paris, the arm had to be amputated.

Too famous to steal, and with only one arm to work with if he hadn't been, Manolesco was rescued by twenty-four-year-old Pauline Tollet, whom he married. He made his last money on a series of articles for Italian newspapers, describing how hotels can keep the property of their guests safe from thieves like him.

In 1911, he died from what has always been deemed a "mysterious and insidious illness." No more information has ever been available.

Mata Hari
1876–1917

The most notorious of all female spies, the personification of the femme fatale, the mysterious exotic and erotic dancer from the East, Mata Hari was really Margaretha Geertruida Zelle, who broke away from her Friesland home in the Netherlands by answering a personal ad in the newspaper placed by lovelorn Dutch Colonial Army Captain Rudolf MacLeod, who was looking for a wife. She married MacLeod in Amsterdam while he was on leave from the East Indies. She was eighteen; MacLeod was forty, and represented escape.

Her father, a wealthy haberdasher, had provided his daughter with a luxurious childhood. He told her she was a special creature and not like other girls. After he lost all his money, Gretha, as she was called, was sent to live with various relatives and got along with none of them. She couldn't cook, wouldn't clean, but was good at daydreaming. She studied to be a kindergarten teacher, but was forced to leave the school after conducting an affair with the headmaster.

She moved to Java with MacLeod, who reverted to his rowdy, bachelor ways and left his young wife to become stultified at home. MacLeod never informed her that he suffered from syphilis. Their son died, possibly of complications from the disease, when he was four years old. Their daughter would outlive Gretha, but died at the age of twenty-one, perhaps from syphilis as well.

IMAGE: Mata Hari, Artist: Anonymous; Photo ID: 42–64341276 © Heritage Images/Corbis. Used with permission.

After five years in the Dutch East Indies, the couple returned to Holland where they divorced in 1903. Gretha took the little girl and tried to earn a living in different Dutch towns, but MacLeod placed ads in the newspapers denouncing her. After he spirited their daughter away, a despondent Gretha boarded the train to Paris. As she later told reporters, "I thought all women who ran away from their husbands went to Paris."

Gretha at first survived on the only skills she had, or thought she had. At the beginning of 1905 she was near destitute, living from trick to trick, but by the end of that year she could pay her $50,000 bill at the jeweller. Her fortunes changed when she got work as an equestrienne with a circus. Gretha was a fine stunt rider, but her boss, circus owner Ernest Molier, suggested she might fare even better as a dancer. So during her time off from the circus, Gretha worked on routines improvised from dances she had studied during her years in the Dutch East Indies.

Gretha—having now adopted her artistic name of Mata Hari —first appeared on March 13, 1905, at the Musée Guimet, an Oriental art museum that housed the collections of wealthy industrialist Émile Guimet. He would later claim that he came up with the "Mata Hari" handle, but the phrase was well known in the East Indies, meaning "the eye of the day." (Back in 1897, Gretha had written to a friend in Holland that she longed to be a dancer, and use the name Mata Hari.) For her dancing debut, she wore a casque of gold upon her head, a breastplate, and a few layers of flimsy cloth. She danced before a statue of Śiva, the Hindu god of destruction and salvation. A correspondent for a London society magazine was present, and was overwhelmed by the show. The writer's first line made her a legend: "Vague rumours had reached me of a woman from the Far East...laden with perfumes and jewels." He ended his review thus: "She divested herself, one by one, of the veils implying that, as a sacrifice, she gave beauty, youth, love, etc.; and finally worked to a frenzy, unclasped her belt and fell in a swoon at Siva's feet."

She was a sensation; that first review captured the romance, the mystery, and the seductiveness of the sex goddess who would in a little over a week be known forever by her new name.

Newspapers and magazines tried to outdo each other in lavishing praise: "majestically tragic, the thousand curves and movements of her body trembling in a thousand rhythms... an exotic spectacle yet deeply austere... Mata Hari dances with her muscles, with her entire body, thus surpassing ordinary methods..."

She danced in theatres, at exclusive salons, and in the homes of the very rich. She danced three times at Natalie Barney's infamous lesbian garden parties at Neuilly-sur-Seine. Mata Hari also had a sideline appearing as Lady Godiva naked on a white horse. She was in the press continually, and offered each interviewer a different story of her life: She was the daughter of a temple dancer, either in Java or India; she was European, stolen as a child and trained to be a dancer; she was rescued from slavery by a Scottish lord who was murdered; she was half-caste; she was of pure Indian blood.

Mata Hari maintained affairs with several highly placed French officials and numerous officers of the military. She went on tour throughout Europe, expanding her fame and her circle of male admirers. In Monte Carlo, she had a brief liaison with opera composer Jules Massenet, and in Berlin became the mistress of the extremely wealthy Alfred Kiepert of the 11th Hussar Regiment. Kiepert set her up in a large home, and when they ended their affair three years later, gave her a small fortune as a farewell present. While in Berlin, she was also the mistress of one of the chiefs of police. In 1906 in Vienna, she engaged in what became known as "the war of the tights" with Isadora Duncan, Maud Allan, and other imitators. Mata Hari vanquished her competitors and declared, "Born in Java, in the midst of tropical vegetation, I have been taught from my earliest childhood the deep meaning of these dances which constitute a cult, a religion. Only those born and bred there become impregnated with their religious significance, and can impart to them that solemn note to which they can lay claim."

As a recent biographer has explained, "She believed her own lies, which was the key to her sincerity."

For several years Mata Hari roamed blithely across the continent, dancing, being lauded by the press, and forming associations with men, most (but not all) of whom were rich. At one time she lived simultaneously in four houses and three apartments given to her by male admirers. She did not, as in earlier days, carry on these affairs for money; she did what she did because, as she never denied, she liked men and she liked having sex with them.

The outbreak of war in 1914 did not at first cause any significant alteration in her manner of living. Although she found it more difficult to move across Europe, the war also meant there were more uniformed men in Paris.

It is unclear when Mata Hari first came to the attention of Allied intelligence, but within a couple of months French detectives were following her night and day. Their reports reveal a woman who, after sending off the man with whom she had spent the night, began a round of shopping, entertained a man for an hour or two in the afternoon, visited more shops, and had another visitor overnight. At one point, while maintaining this schedule, she kept an additional lover, the marquis de Beaufort, in another suite. And none of this kept her from falling in love with a Russian captain, Vladimir de Masloff, who she would claim was the only love of her life.

She was arrested in Paris as a spy on February 13, 1917, and held in horrid conditions until her execution on October 15 of that year. She was forty-one. There has been debate over her guilt or innocence ever since. It is true that she offered herself as a spy to counter-intelligence in France. She explained that her dealings, and sexual relations, with certain highly ranked German officers were the result of her missions for the head of counter-intelligence, Georges Ladoux, who later testified he had not sent her on any such missions. It came down to the word of Ladoux against that of Mata Hari. The latter was—no way around it—an outrageous teller of untruths, and was shown to be so. She was not, however, proved to be a spy. As for Ladoux, four days after Mata Hari was executed, he was exposed as a German agent and imprisoned for treason.

Mata Hari, then, was executed for being a self-described "international woman," who took her pleasures when and with whom she pleased.

The night before her execution, she danced for the two nuns who took care of her and who wanted to remember "the true Mata

Hari," not the wretched, half-starved prisoner they had come to know. She told the sisters that she felt sorry for the soldiers who would always feel the burden of shooting Mata Hari. At 5:00 a.m., dressed in the clothes she had been allowed to wear for her trial—stockings, a two-piece suit, a low-cut blouse, and ankle boots—she tucked her unwashed hair under a tri-cornered hat, set it at a rakish angle, put on gloves, threw a cape around her neck, and declared herself ready. She refused to confess, saying she had done nothing wrong and would not allow the warder to touch her as she made the long walk.

She would not be tied to the stake, refused the blindfold, and waited for the bullets with her hands on her hips.

No one claimed her body. Her head was sent to the Museum of Anatomy in Paris, where the brains of criminals were studied. It later disappeared.

At various times and in subsequent years this audacious
scalawag, this frenetic trickster figure, was a naval surgeon
commander, a bank manager, a major general, an atomic
scientist, a classics professor, Nicholas Monsarrat (the well-known
English novelist), a High Court judge, and a suave ladies' man.

Murray Beresford Roberts 1919–1974

The man's play-acting never seems to have presented itself on the grand stages it deserved or demanded. Manolesco had Monte Carlo, Lustig had Paris, and Weyman had New York, but Murrary Beresford Roberts had to prance, pilfer, and pose far away from the bright lights of famous international locales in Kiwi backwaters and Aussie outback settlements down by the billabong.

Or so it had seemed until recent information surfaced proving that he had impersonated a Lord Standish in Calcutta and made off with a diamond tiara, which a jeweller gave him before receiving payment. It was to be a gift for Lady Standish, who did not exist, but would be arriving from the Himalayas shortly. Up in his suite, Roberts took the tiara apart, swallowed the diamonds, changed taxis three times to get to the airport, flew to Karachi, expelled the diamonds, and got the next flight to London where he sold the jewels for £20,000.

It has also come to light that he had been a borstal boy (a convicted young offender), and there were three years unaccounted for in the United States. But, *otherwise…*

Roberts was born in Wellington, New Zealand, in 1919, an only child of upper-middle-class parents. His father was a surveyor whose best friends were a surgeon and a classics professor, which is important because Murray B. Roberts would impersonate a surgeon and a classics professor at different times in his career. He prepared for the first role by attending the University of Otago medical school for half a year before quitting in boredom, or getting expelled for cheating, depending on the source; he was qualified for the latter role because he had always read prodigiously.

Before spending that short term at the University of Otago, he had done well at grammar school and King's Preparatory School Auckland, where he was remembered as "modest and charming"; alumni also recalled his "soft and persuasive voice." His voice and his charm would serve him well.

The decade beginning in 1938 when he left Otago is veiled in mystery and obscured by contradiction, though it is known that the week after leaving Otago, Roberts passed himself off as a representative for Afghanistan Airways. He enlisted in the Second World War and lasted a month and a half until being released for "psychological abnormality." It is known that his arrest in 1941 for acting as a *locum tenens* for a medical practitioner in Greymouth, New Zealand, was not his first brush with the law. The next year he began serving a two-year prison term for forging a death certificate.

When he got out of prison, Roberts went to New South Wales, Australia, where he obtained various teaching positions after claiming degrees he did not have. When he was fired from a couple of these, Roberts changed his name to John Malcolm Cook and went west. In Kalgoorlie he talked himself into the editorship of the *Kalgoorlie Miner*. He married a typist named Dorothy Elizabeth Bright in 1949, who was either his first or third wife. The newspaper fired him when it learned he was a criminal from New Zealand, and Dorothy filed for divorce for the same reason.

His nefarious activities from 1949 until the end of his life are too many to keep track of. Arrests were frequent, though details are scanty.

In 1951, he was an education officer at Australian Paper Manufacturers Ltd. in Melbourne, and the next year a chemist at Imperial Chemical Industries in Perth—both jobs naturally obtained fraudulently.

In Adelaide, he landed in court in 1952 and was given a three-month sentence for posing as a doctor in the nearby town of Gleneig.

In 1954 in Melbourne, Roberts posed as Professor Sir Leonard Jackson, the new prosecutor for the Petrov royal commission into espionage, which enabled him to obtain credit and money. The next year he was a professor of neurosurgery; as a plastic surgeon he was given entrée to the Goulburn gaol and selected an inmate on whom to perform a skin graft.

In 1956, as a fake homeowner in Tasmania, he relieved a few potential house buyers of their deposits, including the £50 he got from a truck driver named Ernest Stanley Wignall. He then fled to Sydney and passed himself off as Lord Russell, governor-general designate of Australia. He was set up in the best suite in town and ate lavishly until being found out and extradited to Tasmania. He served a few months for his deeds, telling the judge to go easy on him because he was "more of a nuisance...than a criminal."

Upon his release, this "nuisance" posed as Sir William Penny, Sir John Douglas, and Justice Adams—a New Zealand Supreme Court judge. In Melbourne, he was Doctor Bodkin Adams—a real doctor, who the very week that Roberts was portraying him was acquitted in England of murdering two of his patients. Roberts was also, in Sydney, Mr. Law, a wool buyer.

In 1960, also in Sydney, Roberts pulled off a grand charade, acting as German industrialist Baron Alfred von Krupp, and promising to build for the city a £250,000 car park. No sooner was he out of jail for that one than he married Beryl Sinclair, a thirty-one-year-old schoolteacher; eight months later she filed for divorce on the grounds that he had lied on the marriage papers (he had married her as John Martin Jackson).

At various times and in subsequent years this audacious scalawag, this frenetic trickster figure, was a naval surgeon commander, a bank manager, a major general, an atomic scientist, a classics professor, Nicholas Monsarrat (the well-known English novelist), a High Court judge, and a suave ladies' man smooth-talking a series of besotted women out of their savings, their jewellery, and their homes.

In November, 1966, Roberts was arrested at the Bank of New Zealand in Sydney, Australia, just as he was being handed a £4,000 cheque by a widow named Joyce Derrom Brown. Roberts had already taken her for £50,000. They had met in New Zealand and he had impressed her with his background, which included recent diplomatic service in Russia and, previously, command of a ship of the British Navy. She was even more impressed a week later when he declared that for her, he had just refused to accept the post of secretary general of the United Nations. Ms. Brown had accepted all this eagerly, but her relatives had not, and they summoned the law.

As he told the arresting officer: "You have to tell bigger and better stories to keep the interest of the person you are trying to impress."

Not long after being released from prison for that caper, Roberts was teaching *The Illiad* and *The Odyssey* at a girls college in Western Australia.

In 1971, he was sentenced to a mental hospital in Auckland from which he escaped within the week. He was tracked down a few days later in a restaurant in Paihia in the far north of New Zealand just as he was signing an autograph for the waitress, who was a big fan of his novels or, at least, those of Nicholas Monsarrat.

And on and on it went for the three years remaining to him. Murray Beresford Roberts succumbed to alcohol poisoning in 1974 in a rooming house in Papakura, New Zealand, where he had been working on his autobiography. He had assets of £25, and was out on bail for having secured lodging by claiming to be a Supreme Court judge.

His autobiography was published posthumously the following year as *A King of Con Men*, and is, according to reviews, not very reliable.

There is in fact very little reliable information, beyond arrest records and court dates, about Murray Beresford Roberts. More revealing than these facts and figures is a brief account published in *University of Otago* magazine in 2010, under the title "An Alumni Story." It seems that the writer, an Otago graduate, Dr. Ross Smith, had, in 1943, met a Dr. Shearsby on the train from Ltylleton to Dunedin. Smith was about to begin his medical studies and Shearsby, who seemed to know where the young man was going and why, struck up a conversation. Shearsby is described as wearing horn-rimmed glasses and having a "very cultured voice." The older man said he had specialized in neurosurgery abroad before returning to work at Dunedin Hospital.

Besides recommending his former landlady, who would give the young man a room at her boarding house on 357 Great King Street, Shearsby invited Smith to dinner the following evening at Wains Hotel.

But the next night there was no Shearsby at the Wains, and no reservation. Nor did there seem to be a Dr. Shearsby at the Dunedin Hospital. Curious, the young medical student checked twenty years of medical school records and found no one named Shearsby. There was also no 357 Great King Street.

Smith was intrigued enough to persist in the matter, and returned to the hospital the next day to find Dr. Shearsby "in a white coat with a stethoscope around his neck" coming down the stairs. Shearsby told Smith that the staff at the reception desk were new and didn't recognize him.

They arranged to meet the next day, but again Shearsby didn't show up. When Smith explained everything to the hospital manager, the man said, "My God, that could only be Murray Roberts!"

The Fake Formosan and Princess Caraboo 1679–1763 & 1791–1864

The world, it seems, is rife with impostors, most of them dull as dishwater. Guys pretending to be war heroes or drummers in obscure rock bands. Others are more daring, like Ferdinand Waldo Demara and Frank Abagnale Jr., who passed as doctors, airline pilots, preachers, and military officers. Daring they may have been, but scalawags they weren't. Then there was the New Zealander Amy Bock who spent her life being one man after another. She married women who later said they didn't know Amy wasn't a man. Now *that's* faking it.

But even these imposters were amateurs when compared to a very few reckless and imaginative others who invented everything, not only their names and backgrounds, but entire languages and histories of the countries from whence they pretended to hail. Chief among them were two characters known to history, or at least to our peculiar corner of it, as the Fake Formosan and Princess Caraboo. Their real names are a mystery. The only thing certain is that they were confirmed drifters, denizens of the road, and the road is, or was, a place made for fabrication.

The man who would be known as the Fake Formosan was at first an ersatz Irishman walking all over Europe in the early eighteenth century, begging and pretending to be a pilgrim. Having come across a real Irish pilgrim, and speaking neither Gaelic nor English, he decided to stick to Latin, at which he was fluent. But his Latin restricted him to hitting up the clergy and the high-born. Then, thinking it more exotic to be Japanese, he tried that; ignorant of the Japanese language, he invented a gibberish Japanese and, along with it, an entire system of writing.

In the Netherlands, at a fancy dinner party where he was the exotic guest, he met a Reverend Innes from Scotland, who was suspicious of him. After our drifter had entertained with translations of the Bible into "Japanese," Innes invited the young man to call at his residence the next day. There, Innes took down a volume of Cicero and asked for a translation into Japanese. The young man obliged. Innes thanked him and took the book, but then gave it back, asking him to translate the page again. When the two versions did not resemble each other, Innes said something on the order of: "Listen, I know you're a fake, but that's okay. If you're careful, we can make a little money together."

Innes advised him that as it was within the realm of possibility that they might run into an actual Japanese person, he'd best try another Asian country of origin. They settled on Formosa (now Taiwan)—who'd ever been there? (Certainly not Innes, nor the young man.) As well as a new homeland, Innes helped the drifter acquire a new name: George Psalmanazar (in reference to the Biblical King Shalmaneser of Assyria).

The two men hit London in 1703, Psalmanazar claiming he had been kidnapped in Formosa by Jesuit missionaries and taken to France, where he escaped and, luckily, ran into Innes. The pair was fêted at all the best houses where Psalmanazar eschewed the normal fare, dining only on raw meat and roots that had not been washed. He related bizarre stories of his homeland—translated from the "Formosan" by Innes—such as "In my country men are permitted to kill and eat their wives, if suspected of adultery," or "Every year we have a sacrifice of thousands of eight-year-old boys."

After a year of living high, Psalmanazar had attracted doubters, one of them being the astronomer Sir Edmond Halley. To "prove" his assertions, Psalmanazar wrote *Description of Formosa*, a 288-page volume which included discourses on the history, customs, architecture, gastronomy, and religion of Formosa (the fictional Formosan religion having been founded by two philosophers, Zeroaboabel and Chorche Matchin).

Psalmanazar had a run of a few good years, but in 1711 Innes went to Portugal and left him to his own devices. By then Psalmanazar had become a bit of a music hall joke. In 1712, he hooked up with a man named Pattenden, inventor of a whitening lacquer (known incidentally as "japon"), and began marketing chinaware. When this deal didn't work out, he joined the British Army, was discharged for incompetence, and tried to make a go of it by painting decorative fans. After a religious conversion, Psalmanazar wrote a play in Hebrew and became a literary hack. He also became addicted to opium. He mixed it with the pulp of oranges, convinced not only that this cured his addiction, but was a miracle health tonic. Psalmanazar got several of his friends to try his concoction, the result being that he created many new addicts. He met Samuel Johnson, who took a shine to him, and he's mentioned in James Boswell's 1791 book *Life of Samuel Johnson*.

Psalmanazar lived to eighty-four, and until his last days could be seen on the streets of London preaching to strangers about getting right with God. In his desk, after his death, was discovered what purported to be his autobiography: *Memoirs of ****: Commonly Known by the Name of George Palmanazar: A Reputed Native of Formosa*.

In England during the first couple of decades of the 19th century, the police were charged with arresting beggars, rogues, and vagabonds. One young woman in 1817, wearing a turban, was charged with being all three. Evidently what saved her from being bound over was the fact that no one understood what she said. All sorts of people who spoke all sorts of languages listened to her uncomprehendingly. She was eventually taken in by a family named Worrall, and her hosts were given to believe her name was Caraboo. When the girl removed her turban, strange markings could be seen on the back of her head. She recited what seemed to be a prayer before sipping her tea; she became excited upon seeing Chinese characters on furniture.

The Worralls were a respectable pair—Samuel Worrall was a local court magistrate—and it wasn't proper to have an attractive single woman at the house who wasn't a servant; and attractive Caraboo was, with her dark hair and dark eyes, her turbans, and colourful clothes. She was passed from one rooming house and hospital to another. Caraboo marked pieces of paper with strange symbols; she also liked to write in the dirt by the banks of ponds. Her hosts sent some of her writings off to Oxford; they were returned, marked "humbug."

No one could solve the mystery of the young woman's identity. But one day, while walking the road with a keeper, there appeared a traveller who understood her perfectly.

Just as Innes had crossed paths with Psalmanazar, the Portuguese sailor Manuel Enes aided Caraboo. They began chatting away, like old compatriots, to the amazement of Caraboo's guardian. The dark-skinned Enes announced that the girl was a real princess from Javasu, an island in the Indian Ocean. She had been kidnapped by pirates, and was unable to escape until the ship was in the Bristol Channel, where she jumped overboard and swam to shore. She was thus wandering, disoriented, when the police found her in 1817.

Well, people were no longer reluctant to have her in their homes now that she was a princess, but the Worralls prevailed. Visitors enjoyed seeing her dance and climb to the tops of trees to pray to her god, Allah Tallah. She made her own bow and arrows and was skilled at bringing down game to supplement the Worralls' larder. Guests sneaked around the property to glimpse her swimming naked.

Soon the princess was famous throughout the land. But Mrs. Neal, a woman who ran a lodging house in Bristol, read about her in the newspapers, and declared she had rented a room to the girl, who had claimed to be a gypsy. Other people showed up insisting that Caraboo was a prostitute, a beggar, a housemaid, a drunken ne'er-do-well. One fellow insisted he had gotten drunk with her on rum at a roadhouse not long before. The young woman quickly went from being a princess to an embarrassment, and some of that reflected on the Worralls, who shipped her off to that city of fakes and charlatans across the pond in the United States: Philadelphia.

There she was greeted enthusiastically. But after her first couple of months in America, she disappeared, for a little while, to history.

The woman returned to England in 1824 and appeared at theatres on New Bond Street, London, as Princess Caraboo. By the end of the year, she had gone to France and Spain, and perhaps other countries where, evidently, she continued her ruse (if it was indeed a ruse!).

Around 1828, Caraboo was resident at a home for reformed prostitutes. Upon her release, she claimed to have mistaken the place for a nunnery. She then got a job behind the bar at a pub in London, where she became famous for her bizarre stories.

In 1832, calling herself Mary Willcocks (perhaps her true identity), she married Richard Baker, settled down in Bristol, and had a daughter. Her husband didn't stick around long. When she died at age seventy-five, on Christmas Eve, 1864, Princess Caraboo was supporting herself by selling leeches at the Bristol Infirmary Hospital.

But how much of an imposter was Princess Caraboo? Why should the words of a lodging-house owner who had read the girl's description, but hadn't seen a picture of her—much less seen her in person—be trusted more than the words of the traveller Enes? Those who had initially believed her story later professed that she was an obvious fake. Medical experts insisted those curious marks on the back of her head were really the result of cupping operations performed in a London poorhouse hospital, wherein incisions were made in the scalp and covered by egg cups to draw out bad blood. (It should be noted that at the time, many medical experts in England believed that one Mary Toft, of Guildford, just up the road from Bristol, had indeed given birth to seventeen rabbits.)

If Princess Caraboo was really a poor, homeless girl, addle-brained since childhood, how and where had she learned to make bows and arrows? And as for Enes, what of him?

For that matter, what of his predecessor Innes?

(Princess Caraboo was the subject of a movie released in 1994. In real life, she was a fantastic character surrounded by dullards. In this movie, the bit players steal the show from the actress playing the princess, who resembles a dime-a-dozen airhead from the mall. Fortunately, the Formosan imposter has, so far, eluded blandization on the screen.)

How did Psalmanazar and Caraboo pull it off? Where did they come from, and who were they? Just a couple of drifters with imaginations too big for their surroundings, eager for more than life seemed to offer?

CONSTANTINE SAMUEL RAFINESQUE.

Constantine Rafinesque
1783–1840

In 1818, a strange-looking fellow in his mid-thirties, of no readily discernible origin who spoke English with an indefinable accent, alighted on the shore of the Ohio River at Henderson, Kentucky. The man had begun this particular trip in Philadelphia on borrowed money, reaching Henderson by a runabout route covering two thousand miles. He had been contracted to survey and map the Ohio River, and collect information about the landscape and towns all the way to the Wabash River. A naturalist and botanist, the man identified one hundred new fish en route, thereby increasing the number of known fish in America by twenty per cent. From Pittsburgh

IMAGE: Constantine Rafinesque, courtesy *Transylvania University*.

91

to Cincinnati he travelled on a flat-bottomed boat, walked one hundred miles to Louisville, and caught a keel boat to Henderson. On shore, he sat down, removed his shoes, and called to a man nearby, "Where might I find John J. Audubon?"

"You've found him," said the stranger.

Everyone has heard of Audubon, but how many are familiar with the name of his visitor, the greatest naturalist and botanist of his day and, perhaps, the greatest in North American history? He was Constantine Samuel Rafinesque—at the time much better known than Audubon, but infamous rather than famous.

Audubon would later delight in describing Rafinesque's appearance, his plant-stained yellow coat, tight pants, scraggly beard, and shoulder-length hair; he had holes in his socks, and his only luggage consisted of a case filled with plant specimens, dead birds, and fossils.

"My dear Audubon, I send you an odd fish which you may prove to be indescribable."

"And where might I find this odd fish?"

"You've found him," said Rafinesque.

No one has ever accused Audubon of being a kindly fellow, so it is not surprising that he took advantage of the funny-looking visitor's naïveté, first getting him lost, and later describing a mythical fish—the devil-jack diamond—to Rafinesque, who would later write a scholarly account of it ("This may be reckoned the wonder of the Ohio.... The whole body covered with large stone scales...they strike fire with steel! and are ball proof!"). Audubon proceeded to relate his ruse to fellow naturalists, and everyone had a great laugh at Rafinesque's expense. They were used to doing that kind of thing, and Rafinesque was used to being the victim of that kind of thing. But he was smarter than all of them, and probably everyone else, too.

Known in America as "The Italian" or "The Greek," he was of French and German heritage, born in Constantinople in 1783. He grew up in Marseille speaking French and Greek (his mother had been raised in Athens). His father died when the boy was nine years old, and he was taken by his mother to Italy where they stayed four years, during which time Rafinesque later claimed to have read "a thousand books," and wrote his first long essay, "Notes on the Apennines."

They returned to Marseille, where he continued his omnivorous reading, and by the age of fourteen he had completed, among other works, the six-volume, forty-five-thousand-page *Dictionnaire Raisonné Universal D'Histoire Naturelle*. He was a solitary youth who never attended school, but spent his time with tutors or wandering alone. He never went to church, either; he realized early on that his religion did not exist indoors, but out of doors.

In 1802, Rafinesque's mother gave him passage to America where he might find work. The young man disembarked at Philadelphia, then the largest and most important city in the United States. He was offered a job by Benjamin Rush, the top physician in America and a signatory of the Declaration of Independence, but turned him down. It was not a move destined to advance his career. Instead, Rafinesque obtained employment with a mercantile outfit that allowed him to travel and botanize. Although ordinary people would reject Rafinesque's company, he made friends easily among the less respectable and eccentric ones. He soon hooked up with Thomas Forrest, a Revolutionary War veteran and future congressman (who assumed the dress of a Quaker and was forever switching political parties). Together they roamed the countryside studying plants and animals. On one of these trips, Rafinesque encountered his first Indian and began what was to be a lifetime of studying everything about native people. It was the first of many extensive walking trips and, on another the following year, he acquired an interest in snakes and reptiles, becoming one of the first American herpetologists.

Once in Washington, he spent a day with President Jefferson, who he managed to irritate by correcting the great man, thus dashing his hopes of going out on the Lewis and Clark Expedition. To further make acceptance impossible and publication nearly so, Rafinesque was vocal in condemning slavery and America's treatment of its native people. In order to survive, Rafinesque left for Italy in 1805 with his large collection of botanical specimens.

He arrived in March, and after a few weeks exploring, settled in Palermo, Sicily, where he got work as secretary to the American consul, proving himself invaluable since he by then spoke eight or nine languages. As well, Rafinesque started a business selling medicinal plants and what he called "squibs," the bulbs of sea onions which were dried and promoted as a tonic and diuretic. He was also big on barilla, a category of sea plants that could be used in the manufacturing of soda, soap, and glass. He made a lot of money and bought a house in Palermo, but quit his job at the consulate to go wandering. He collected sea plants and molluscs and wrote about them in Italian. As well, he turned out articles on quarantine practices in Sicily, fumigation techniques in France, medicinal plants, and European plants that had been adapted in America. In 1809, he set off to explore all of Sicily by mule. He met up with a mountain bandit and travelled with him for a couple of weeks.

Rafinesque underwent numerous business setbacks which he never discussed at length, but it seems that too many Sicilian politicians had their hands out. He was also unlucky in love. Only after his death was it discovered that Rafinesque had married, in 1809, and fathered a daughter (who later achieved minor success as an actress) and son, who died in infancy. His wife Josephine Vaccaro was unfaithful, and Rafinesque took ship to return to the United States in 1815. It is somehow simultaneously sad and hilarious that his wife immediately married a comedian.

In early August, 1815, his ship Union was wrecked off Long Island and he lost all his belongings—fifty boxes containing drugs, his manuscripts, 20,000 species, "cabinet collections and part of my library, 2,000 maps and drawings, 300 copper plates, a shell collection with 60,000 specimens"—as well as nearly all his money. He later wrote that while swimming to shore, he had the presence of mind to notice "several new genera and species of fish and aquatic plants." (One is sure that Josephine Vaccaro's new husband could have gotten good material out of that image.)

It is certain that many of Rafinesque's American colleagues did find humour in this latest misfortune.

Rafinesque angered the scientific establishment by claiming dozens of new species and ignoring the accepted classification systems of Linnaeus and Jussieu. It got worse for him when he expounded his belief that plants and animals evolved, which was, of course, directly opposed to the beliefs of the fundamentalists who declared everything was as it had always been, as God created it. His detractors were employed by universities, libraries, and museums—a group of people known as "closets"—while Rafinesque was a field man, the field being a place where most of the closets had never been. But the closets controlled the publications, and consequently Rafinesque was rarely able to get his work published in America. His first published work on the changing of species appeared in France in 1817, although he had held the belief since he was a teenager.

He spent a long spell of dire hustling; a brief respite occurred when he obtained a Quaker patron who staked him to an exploration trip along the upper Hudson River. But the closets continued to snub him when he tried again to publish. All his claims and discoveries were ignored or discredited. He identified a new vine and called it Bradurya after a collector friend. A year later, an establishment botanist, Thomas Nutall, renamed the plant after Caspar Wistar, his college professor, and thus the vine has ever since been know as wisteria.

It was at this point that Rafinesque borrowed money and began his long trek west, during which he met Audubon. In Lexington, he encountered an old friend who got him a job teaching at Transylvania University, the first university west of the Allegheny Mountains. It was necessary for Rafinesque to trek all the way back to Philadelphia to see to his affairs and possessions, and then trek all the way back to Lexington, which he did, collecting and studying Indian mounds as he went.

He began teaching at Transylvania in the autumn of 1819 as professor of botany and natural history and professor of modern languages. The administration, aware of his passion for his own studies, decided they could save money by denying Rafinesque a salary. He was given room and board, firewood, and candles. The students liked him for his eccentricity. The townsfolk didn't know what to think of him because he was a new species to them. To earn an income, he gave lectures to the public on moral philosophy, metaphysics, zoology, agriculture, philology, education, Free Masonry for women, and the Greek-Turkish situation.

He was at Transylvania for six years and kept himself busy. Besides teaching, lecturing, and walking over the mountains to Philadelphia and back every summer, Rafinesque found time to invent a way to measure objects by dumping them in water. He also invented a method of fireproofing architecture, a steam plow, artificial leather, and a shallow water navigation system.

Rafinesque wrote papers listing five successive civilizations that had settled America, the first coming from North Africa. It was necessary to publish these himself. After his death, it was discovered that while at Lexington he composed twelve long poems to twelve women, never identified. He also promoted the raising of mulberry bushes and the farming of silkworms. He pushed for a public garden in Lexington, and the town government not only agreed to its installation, but made Rafinesque the superintendent.

Compared to Rafinesque, most polymaths seem like single-minded plodders. On August 23, 1825, he was granted a patent for what he called the "Divital System of Banking." For a fee, any bank might adopt this system, which basically allowed patrons to deposit anything of value. He believed that banks should create wealth for the benefit of society, an idea as abhorrent then to the powers-that-be as it would be now. To explain his system and the theory behind it, Rafinesque later published two books: *Safe Banking Including the Principles of Wealth* (1837) and *Pleasures and Duties of Wealth* (1840).

He spent the rest of that summer setting up his own Divital Bank of Philadelphia, and got back to Lexington to find his room had been broken into and possessions scattered or missing. When Rafinesque complained, he was fired. He put a curse on the president and the school, mailed his remaining stuff to Philadelphia, and set off by shank's mare.

Fortunately, a friend in the wealthy suburb of Germantown

permitted Rafinesque to stay in his home, because by the time he had beat his way back east, he was flat broke. It would be five years before he was able to gather enough money to get his remaining books and papers out of storage. As if things weren't bad enough, Rafinesque contracted tuberculosis. He declined medical treatment and cured himself with a concoction he put together from mixing and crushing various vegetables. He was encouraged to market this mess, which he called Pulmel, boasting that it was a preventative and effective treatment for consumption. It was obtainable as Wine of Pulmel, and Sugar of Pulmel; as a pill, a lozenge, syrup, or as a chocolate drink. One could also purchase a concentrated Pulmel ("Dose one grain but double the price"). He was the living proof that it worked.

His patent medicine being successful, Rafinesque was encouraged to set himself up as a sort of mail-order doctor. One could write to him with one's symptoms and he would suggest a treatment. He took a holistic approach to medicine and encouraged his patients to get exercise and avoid fatty foods, salt, and sugar. Again he was ahead of his time, and as usual the specialists denounced him; the medical establishment tried to put him out of business.

All this time, he was writing about native peoples, their origins, and languages. As well as being a pioneer in this field, Rafinesque was one of the first to explore phonology, the study of sounds in language. He proved that abstract ideas were expressed in Indian languages and in symbols. This was greeted by his enemies as being absurd. Rafinesque is the first person on record to attempt to decipher Mayan hieroglyphics.

For many years, as a result of his studies in the languages, customs, and history of the native peoples of America, Rafinesque had been working on an epic tale of the Lenape Indians (now known as the Delaware). Near the end of his life, he produced a vast chronicle he called the *Walam Olum*, a story that called to mind the great epics of history. It covered three thousand years and encompassed creation, flood, migration, settlement, and culture. Rafinesque claimed that a man he called Doctor Ward of Indiana, whom he'd met on the trail, made him a gift of Lenape talking sticks and tablets, and it was from these that he translated the *Walam Olum*.

Naturally, self-professed experts in the field of Indian studies declared that the work was a hoax, which just went to prove what all the experts in other fields had said about Rafinesque: he was nuts.

(In 1954, more than a hundred years after Rafinesque's death, a team of investigators including anthropologists, archaeologists, ethnographers, and linguists, under the auspices of the Indiana Historical Society, concluded a twenty-year study of the *Walam Olum*, and determined that it was an authentic document. In 1994, however, a man named David M. Oestreicher published an article in the *Bulletin of the Archaeological Society of New Jersey* titled, "Unmasking the Walam Olum: A 19th Century Hoax." To this day, Rafinesque's studies remain controversial.)

In 1832, Rafinesque set out his theory of evolution in full. Charles Darwin paid tribute to him in *On the Origin of Species*, published in 1859. Rafinesque's American colleagues thought he was crazy. A feeling that was expressed with vitriol when in 1836 Rafinesque published his long poem, *The World: or, Instability*, which was part hymn to the great changeability of the living world, and part nature mysticism. The last thing the establishment of the time would ever tolerate was a wandering nature bard proclaiming that he was as one with the flora and the fauna. He was attacked by the creationists, laughed at, and shunned.

Rafinesque spent most of his remaining years roaming the countryside, pursuing his first love of natural history, and stopping occasionally to practise medicine. He was ruined by the financial crisis of 1837; there were innumerable bank failures, including that of his Divital Bank of Philadelphia. Near destitute again, Rafinesque grew ill and was diagnosed with stomach and liver cancer. Contrary to long-accepted myth, his last days were not spent in a rooming house where he hadn't paid his rent for months, nor were his body and possessions smuggled out of the building by acquaintances to avoid creditors. Rafinesque had a place to stay in a comfortable home of friends of modest means. True to his nature, he refused the doctor's use of calomel, which was common treatment for cancer in those days. Also true to his nature, he was right. Calomel, or mercury(I) chloride, is poisonous.

Considering the life and personality of Constantine Rafinesque, it is not surprising that his story does not end with his death in 1840. Although he had wished to be cremated because he didn't want his body "to contaminate the earth and possibly be the cause of disease to other men," he was, in fact, buried in a cemetery in Philadelphia in a section called Stranger's Field. In 1924, the librarian of Transylvania University decided to have his body exhumed and sent to the university in Kentucky. In 1840, American burial practice was to bury bodies one on top of another, there usually being five or six bodies to a grave. Initially, there was some confusion about the ordering of bodies in Rafinesque's grave, and the skeleton of one Mary Passmore was sent to Transylvania University by mistake. After a while, the mix-up of remains was discovered— one clue being that Rafinesque's skull had been opened during his autopsy in order to ascertain the cause of his strangeness—and the correct skeleton—Rafinesque's—eventually made its way to his tomb in the university's Old Morrison building.

There is a long-standing tradition at Transylvania University of celebrating Rafinesque Week at Halloween; students get inebriated at the downstairs grill, called "The Rafskellar"—a pun on the word Rathskellar, in the Mitchell Fine Arts Building. One year they even stole Rafinesque's skeleton.

But what about the abrupt firing of Rafinesque from Transylvania University and that curse he put on the president and the school? Six months after the curse was levelled, the president dropped dead, and six months after that most of the university was destroyed by fire. It has only recently been discovered that Rafinesque was having an affair with the president's wife.

Renton Nicholson
1809–1861

Surely there were days when the gods and goddesses of outrage, of the con, the gaff, and the hell-bent-for-leather ludicrous enterprise rested from their misdeeds, and lay fallow to plot the next creative act. Wilson Mizner must have occasionally put his cards away and his feet up and listened to radio; Eliza Lynch undoubtedly paused in her plundering; even Ignaz Trebitsch-Lincoln had to have had a day when he didn't know who the hell he was.

Renton Nicholson, however, eventually known as "Lord Chief Baron," never rested. He was on the hustle from the age of four until the day he died at fifty-two, all day, every day. He didn't install himself as king of any tropical isle, but ruled a twilight kingdom of blacklegs and flash, the other side of the official Victorian world. And everything he did, honest or not, was imbued or described with a language as adventurous as his life.

Born in 1809 on the outskirts of London, he was barely out of nappies when both parents died. He was raised for a time by his brother and sisters in Islington. By the time he was able to walk, young Renton, who was a chubby fellow and stayed that way, was prowling the vicinity, attracted to the action on the street and in the taverns. His siblings sent him to school for a couple of years. The headmaster was a Henry Butter and Renton's teacher was a

IMAGE: "Lord Chief Baron" Renton Nicholson presiding over the crowd in Garrick's Head in Bow Street. Illustration from Warrick Wroth, *Cremorne and the Later London Gardens.*

Mr. Cheesely. A big event in his early life was when he sneaked into a tavern behind his grown-up brother and sat under the table while the young men held a mock court, trying one of their gang for wearing outrageous attire on Easter day.

Figuring the boy was educated enough by age twelve, his sisters apprenticed him for three years to a pawnbroker. There, under the sign of "the swinging dumplings," young Renton gained an early and intense look at life and character. He also made friends who would last a lifetime, one of them being the popular pugilist and later heavyweight champion of England, Jem Ward. This worthy sport had a woman friend who, in Nicholsonese, was a "crapulous constituent of Bacchus." She was in the habit of stealing, or "impignorating," Ward's clothes to pawn in order to buy booze.

Due to his employ, the boy often had to appear in court as a witness. There, his interest in the law, or the theatre of it, kindled by the experience with his brother, was stoked anew.

His "master" didn't live on the shop premises, hence Renton was free to spend his nights in dives, becoming acquainted with magsmen and skittle-sharps, and all manner of rounders and rascals. He learned the rudiments of gambling and chicanery. He was adept at dice in the box, which he called "children in the wood," and was known to handle the "grey"—coins with two heads or two tails. When his apprenticeship was done, he spent a few years moving from one pawnshop to another, each in a different part of London, and each servicing a different class of clientele. At a pawnshop in Leicester Square during the daytime, he got his first glimpse of the gentry in distress, and at gambling parlours in the evenings, he saw the ones who weren't. This perspective of Victorian society prompted him, while still in his teens, to coin an immortal phrase: "One half of the world doesn't know how the other half lives."

Nicholson had a keen mind, a sharp eye, and an ear tuned to language and song. He amassed an incomparable knowledge of this empire of infamy. As well, he was charming, immensely likeable, and had the gift of the gab. But unlike so many great raconteurs, he was also a great listener. His circle of friends and enemies was enormous, both sharps and flats (rounders and squares). Some of these, from the roster of the former, included Frosty-Faced Fogo, the Lively Kid, Standing Sam, Sing-Song Phillips, and the highly put-upon eccentric anti-cleric Robert Taylor. Others whom Nicholson later described in newspapers became less interesting characters when appearing in official literature, such as his intemperate pal William Maginn, a classical scholar of questionable ethics who appears as Captain Shandon in William Thackeray's novel *Pendennis*.

It somehow seems incredible that Renton Nicholson avoided prison until he reached the relatively advanced age of twenty-two, when he was sent to debtors' prison for incurring significant debts after his jewellery store went bankrupt. When asked years later by a journalist if he remembered the exact date of this event, he replied, "Remember it well, it was two days after the fight between Young Dutch Sam and Ned Neal ... January 18, 1831." After a pause he added, "Ephraim Bond and his brother Robert, who had a cork leg, surrendered the same night ... "

You can just hear that line delivered by W.C. Fields.

Released from King's Bench Prison two months later, Nicholson slept in doorways in St. James Square for several days until rescued by a dying streetwalker. By the time she had passed on, several weeks later, Nicholson had hustled the money to pay for her funeral. He survived as a pool shark and ballad maker. He wrote the epitaph for Blind Jack Dawes, a fellow prisoner, and a name familiar to contemporary pop music fans from Tom Waits's song "Walking Spanish."

Nicholson's popularity as a word slinger spread, and he made some money selling songs, and squibs to newspapers. He is also responsible for what is probably the best stanza of boxing verse ever produced, an ode to pugilist Owen Swift, recalling his vicious encounter with Anthony Noon, who died a few days later:

The Gods to prove their hero still
An offspring of their might,
Gave him the science, the skill
To turn Noon into Night.

At age twenty-seven, he married an eighteen-year-old girl and opened a cigar shop, running a card game in the back room. After a couple of months, he was busted again for not having a gambling licence. He was flat broke when he was released in 1837, but soon began working as the editor of *The Town*, a paper that under his direction chronicled the lives and adventures of members of London's high society.

While still in his thirties, Nicholson was already lamenting the passing of a golden age of flash and hustle. In reference to the old St. Giles area of London, he wrote, "It was a city of refuge for the desperado, the thief, the cadger and the prostitute. It now scarcely affords a home for the latter two classes."

After his next stint in the joint, this time the Queen's Prison in 1840—convicted of libel by a jury of men he had criticized in his newspaper—he became owner of Garrick's Head and Town Hotel where he established the Judge and Jury Society, which was soon notorious—a notoriety that would immortalize Renton Nicholson. Over the next twenty years, the society would be incarnated in several other locales. It presented a mock courtroom situation, a grand piece of theatre that had been forming in Nicholson's brain since that day he sneaked into the tavern behind his brother. There were defendants, lawyers for the prosecution and defence, juries, and onlookers. Some of these players were real judges and lawyers. Some defendants had been real defendants, getting a chance to reprise their roles. Soon people were waiting in line in the streets to get into "court." These mock trials made fun of popular current ones; some were restaged famous trials of the past; they were scurrilous, scandalous, indecent, and satirical. Nicholson, dressed in a judge's wig and robe and addressed as "my lord" by the players, delighted in presiding and speechifying. So popular did his bogus baron character become, that in his frequent appearances in real courtrooms he was referred to as Lord Chief Baron Nicholson. The popular society was demanded in the provinces, and Nicholson took his show on the road, enlisting real actors, street people, and local celebrities.

Eventually he expanded his show, adding food and drink, *tableaux vivants* and what were probably the original *poses plastiques*.

The first of these "living pictures" featured scenes from famous paintings recreated by actors and dramatically lighted. But the *poses plastiques* were solely a product of Nicholson's febrile and basically anarchistic mind. English law strictly prohibited the movement or speech of naked people on stage. Nicholson realized, however, that the law said nothing about naked people standing still and silent, and soon he had Eve, Aphrodite, Cleopatra, and the like impersonated by naked chorus girls.

Crowds were so large that Nicholson realized it made no economic sense to stage the Judge and Jury Society and the *poses plastiques* on the same bill—he could have a sold-out house with either one. It happens that besides his roles as impresario, Lord Chief Baron, balladeer, and newspaperman, Nicholson also hit the racing circuit in season, setting up gambling tents, dancing booths, and stands that served food and drink. So it was to this branch of his travelling empire he added a tent for the *poses plastiques*.

He made a fortune during his last years, and gave it all away, just as in earlier days he gave away whatever coins found their way to his pockets to many poor Londoners.

Nicholson was in and out of jail from 1840 until his death in 1861 on charges ranging from debt and libel, to operating a gaming club without a licence. In-between jail, he wrote political speeches, recited his ballads in taverns, and was the poet laureate of London's Drury Lane theatre.

In 1860, he wrote *Rogue's Progress: The Autobiography of "Lord Chief Baron" Nicholson*.

On the day before his death at age fifty-two in 1861, Nicholson was released from yet another stint in lock-up. He went directly from jail to preside over his court at the Coal Hole tavern. The very next evening, while dressing for his performance, he fell down dead. The immediate cause of death was listed as dropsy, as a result of congestive heart failure.

Even the "straight" press noted his passing. One newspaper described him as "humorous, handsome, obese, sensual, impudent; a rooker of the rich and the soul of good nature to the poor." Another obit writer sniffed, "A man of real talent and geniality gone hopelessly along the wrong track."

Uncle "Bull"
1917–?

"I was with the Legion, fighting the Rifs. Those are your white Eh-rabs in Morocco. This would have been in '46."

The words came from my latest uncle, William Caradine, my aunt Louise's new husband. I think he was the third one, or maybe the fourth. He insisted I call him "Uncle Bill." They had just gotten married and were living in my aunt's house in Virginia, near Richmond. We, my parents and I, had travelled south for a week. When I thought everyone was asleep, I'd go downstairs, make coffee, and watch the late late movie. I was thirteen; it was 1958. The movie that night was *Beau Geste*.

"That's how it looked, too," he said, pointing a fat thumb at the screen. "Then after North Africa, I got sent to Southeast Asia. We could have wiped out those Communists in a New York minute, but the trouble was all the officers were French regulars who'd spent the war years sitting on their fannies in Vichy, but most of the new recruits had been with the German army. America's over there now, but you don't hear about it in the newspapers."

"So I guess you speak French, right, Uncle Bill?"

He said something that could have been French, but what did I know? "Yes sir, French. Eye-talian. Portuguese, Spanish, and a little Tamil and some Mandarin I picked up when I was a spy in Asia."

IMAGE: The only known photograph of William Caradine; he is pictured with high school faculty members and seated in the front row, second from left, wearing a bow tie.

"You were really a spy?"

He glanced at the staircase, looked back at me, and whispered, "Yeah, but I can't talk about it. It would upset your aunt. A fine woman."

I had known my aunt as a no-nonsense, conservatively dressed single woman. But now it was as if she had gone into a room and come out an entirely different person: makeup, bouffant hair, green high-heeled shoes, laughing all the time, and always kissing with Uncle Bill. She had danced all night at the wedding reception, shaking her sequined rear end. I saw them on the metal folding chairs, Uncle Bill's hand halfway up her skirt, and her skirt ending above her knees to begin with. Some way for a minister to act, I thought. And that's what he was: pastor of the biggest Baptist church in this town near Richmond.

"So when did you turn to religion, Uncle Bill?"

"November 14, 1952, in the jungle in Indo-China. I saw God in the lianas. Got down on my knees and accepted him into my life or, rather, I gave my life to Him and His son, Jesus Christ. And He immediately lifted my burdens as if He was taking my packsack off my weary back, and He pointed out the way I had to go. Course it took a lot of effort for me to keep on the path and stay the course."

Brian Donlevy was onscreen, marching back and forth flicking that riding crop, looking evil with his moustache. Uncle Bill jerked his head in Donlevy's direction, just as the major, or whatever he was, gave some crazy order. "That fellow looks like he knows what he's doing. Looks like the real thing, not like some of these pretty boys they got in the movies nowadays. I used to work in films when I was a young man. Nothing to brag about; I won't lie to you. Mostly I did stunts: ride horses, fall off horses, get shot and tumble off roof tops. Was born in Wyoming; grew up on a ranch near Elk Creek. So I was practically raised on a horse. Got to know a lot of those actors. Actresses, too. Yvonne De Carlo, yum yum. But don't tell your aunt I mentioned that."

"Okay. Did you know any of the cowboys? Like John Wayne and Jimmy Stewart?"

"I knew the Duke pretty well. Used to go to his place for barbecue, but he stopped inviting me on account of his wife took a shine to me. She was a Mexican or Puerto Rican or something."

"How about Randolph Scott?"

"Hah! Randy! Well, I'll let you in on a little secret about Randolph Scott. He, well ... he liked, well, never mind. Say, I'm going to get me a little drink of whisky. You want a tad in your coffee?"

"Sure, Uncle Bill."

We stayed in Virginia a couple more days, and I would watch the late late movie, and both nights, once my aunt was asleep, Uncle Bill came down, got out the bourbon and poured me a "tad," as he called it, and we'd watch the movie and I'd listen to him talk. One night it was a gangster picture, and he mentioned that he had been close to the Purple Gang. The other night it was a mystery, and he said that the female star was not as good-looking as his first wife, who'd died tragically in a four-car collision.

We started home the next morning, my parents and I, and were hardly out of the driveway when my father said, "Christ, that Bill Caradine is full of it, huh?"

My mother shook her head. "I think he's disgusting. Thinks he knows everything. I don't understand what my sister sees in him."

"I like Uncle Bill," I said.

"Uncle Bull is more like it," said my father.

"I like his stories."

"Yeah," my father grunted. "You can like his stories, just don't believe any of them. Like the one about him playing minor league ball. Could have made the majors, he says, if it weren't for getting stabbed outside a nightclub in Harlem. Of course he beat up both guys. Majors my ass."

"Chris!" my mother said.

"Sorry."

Hell, it hadn't even occurred to me that his stories might not be true. Not that I was naïve. I had already run away from home and had adventures of my own and caused my parents plenty of grief. But the thing I dug about Uncle Bill was that he never once asked me if I liked school or if I played on any teams. He didn't ignore me, either. He talked to me like I was another guy his age. The only other adult I'd ever met who treated me that way was an aristocratic Russian tramp I'd met at Niagara Falls—but that's another story.

Aunt Louise had married Bill Caradine in the winter; the following summer they came north to visit us, Uncle Bill wheeling a '58 Ford convertible, the brand new model where the top retracted into the trunk. He climbed out of the car wearing khakis, a Hawaiian shirt, and shades. Aunt Louise had on shades too, and there seemed to be fifteen pounds less of her. He strutted up the walkway to the house, a big guy with a big head, big hands, and a big nose, his moll behind him. What he didn't look like was a pastor.

The four adults sat around the living room with highballs. Uncle Bill looked at me, then at his glass, and winked, as if to say, Don't worry, you'll get a tad later.

One of the neighbours came over—he worked in a bank—and I could tell Uncle Bill was bored. He started rubbing his leg, then finally stood up and said, "My legs are cramped up after all that driving. If no one minds, I think'll take a little walk, loosen them up."

Then he looked at me. "Jimmy, you want to show me the elephant?"

I got his drift, but no one else did. We walked a couple of blocks down to the main intersection of the town. I led him to the garage. Old Mick, the mechanic who sometimes talked to me, was bent over the hood of a '62 Chrysler fiddling with the carburetor. He nodded to me and to Uncle Bill. After a minute of listening to the carburetor, Bill said, "If you don't mind me saying so, I don't think you're going to get the mixture right however you set it. I think you got to reset the gaps on the spark plugs."

Old Mick glared at him. "Uh huh."

Bill took the hint and we walked away, him telling me about different cars he'd had, and about entering old wrecks in demolition derbies when he was a younger man. "Last year, had to sell my pride and joy, a '47 Chevy Fleetline, you know the fastback model. Had a Corvette engine in it, dual four-barrels; it was lowered, chopped, and channelled, and I louvred the hood. Inside was rolled and pleated. Louise convinced me it wasn't the proper sort of car for a minister of the Lord to be seen in."

When we got to the trolley station, he asked me where it went.

"Philadelphia," I told him.

"Don't you sometimes just want to get on that trolley and go to the end of the line and get on the next one and keep on going and so forth and so on?"

"Yes, sir." And I told him how earlier that year I had done that very same thing.

He laughed and his big belly shook.

"God damn, boy. I still want to do something like that. But I have a responsibility to my flock. And to your aunt Louise."

We went into a couple of stores, but he seemed too big for them, and the shop clerks and other shoppers seemed colourless. It was like he was from another planet.

By the time we got back, the neighbour had gone, my mother was huddled with her sister, and my father had vanished, probably to avoid Uncle Bill. I had to go to a baseball game. Bill was left to sit out of place on a chair in the living room. As I was going out the kitchen door, I heard my aunt say to my mother, "I tell you, Kathleen!" in this low growl that came from the back of her throat. They both giggled.

The next day my father was going to play golf; Uncle Bill invited himself along; I went too. In the car, Uncle Bill said, "I was a professional golfer years ago. Club pro in Roanoke."

My father said, "Isn't there anything you haven't done?"

There was certainly an edge to it.

"Nope," Uncle Bill said, staring straight ahead out the window.

My father had his clubs and I had my own set—half lefties, half righties—and Uncle Bill had to rent a set. They made a fifty-buck bet on the game.

While Bill was in the clubhouse, my father said, "Now I'm going to shut his mouth for good."

Bill's first shot off the tee went about fifty yards straight ahead before looping another hundred yards into the woods to the right of the fairway. He shook his head and examined the shaft of his driver.

"I don't think it's the club," my father said.

Bill smiled, teed up another ball, and hit it about three hundred yards straight down the fairway.

"You were right," he said to my father.

Well, a novel could be written about that game of golf, and not a sports story either. The result was that my father shot an 82, me a 90, and Uncle Bill an 80, winning the fifty dollars. But worse than that, from my father's perspective, was that at least ten of Uncle Bill's shots were either amateurish hooks and slices, or feeble dribbles off the tee. Subtract those and Uncle Bill would have killed my father's score. As it were, my old man threw his bag into the trunk, the clubs clattering. He slammed the trunk lid, and then slammed the car door, and didn't say a word to Uncle Bill the rest of the visit.

That night over our whiskies, in front of our movie, Bill tried to appear contrite: "It probably wasn't fair," he said. "I used to hustle golf. I'm losing my touch. I shouldn't have hit that perfect drive off the first tee. Should have flubbed more shots and then if I was really hustling, I would have asked your father if he wanted to raise the bet. Maybe religion saved me, but ruined me, too."

As they were leaving the next day, Bill gave me a Roman coin that he said he'd found in a farmer's field in Virginia.

I never saw him again.

When I next saw Old Mick, the garage mechanic, he said, "That old corn-pone fellow you was with, son of a bitch was right about the spark plug gaps."

Two years later, Uncle Bill was fired from his job as head preacher at the Baptist church. It seems he was conducting affairs with several of the women in his congregation. He and my aunt got a divorce. During the course of the investigation, it was discovered he hadn't the degree in theology from Bob Jones University that he claimed to have, nor had he been ordained.

Louise continued to keep tabs on Uncle Bill. It seems that he had absconded with Wyatt Earp's six-shooter, which had been in our family since my great uncle Ike Clanton took it off Wyatt in a fist fight out back of the theatre in Tombstone, a few months before the notorious, so-called gunfight. Anyway, in 1963 my aunt mailed a clipping to my mother about how Bill Caradine was fired from his job as a professor of Economics at the local junior college, having obtained his position through fraud. He didn't have a doctorate from Vanderbilt, after all.

My aunt got married again in 1965 to Curtis Williams, who owned a few furniture stores and was a genuinely nice man. He hired a private detective to trace Earp's gun, and perhaps thereby catch the con man trying to sell the thing.

One evening in 1966, a woman in her mid-twenties showed up at the Williams residence and announced she was the daughter of Bill Caradine, her estranged father. Aunt Louise didn't know her former husband had any children. The woman explained that her father had left the family—her, her mother, and sister—one night in 1956 with no explanation. Home had been in Colorado Springs, Colorado, where Uncle Bill worked as a ski instructor. They never heard from him again. When this woman reached her twenties, she hired a private investigator to find traces of the scoundrel.

Neither her private eye, nor Williams's, uncovered a trace of Bill Caradine.

The last rumour I heard had Uncle Bill working as a marine insurance investigator in Charleston, South Carolina. Then he just vanished.

Jack Donovan
1894–1981

Uncle "Bull" wasn't the only scalawag I had the honour of meeting personally. The other day I was thinking of my old pal Jack Donovan, long gone now, a true wastrel who strutted resolutely through the halls of infamy. Every now and again something gets me thinking about him and this time it happened while I was watching *The Treasure of the Sierra Madre* on video. Bogart's on the bum in Tampico and he keeps hitting up the same guy, played by John Huston, the director himself in a white linen suit. Jack could have played Huston, the big-shot gringo south of the border, or Jack could have been the Bogart character, Fred. C. Dobbs.

Anyway, when Jack Donovan appears at the back of my mind he invariably shoulders his way to the front, says something like, "Hey, get the Caddy going and let's head on down to Laguna Beach. Whattaya say?"

I don't know why I never did it before, but only just the other day I checked him out on the Internet. I suppose I had wanted the memory of that scalawag to stay as it was, and not be tarnished by facts and figures and reality. Most of all I didn't want to find out that his stories were not true. But then, maybe, I told myself with a bit of hope, he is not even represented by Uncle Google.

IMAGE: Jack out on the town with Jean Harlow, 1933. (from *Harlow in Hollywood: The Blonde Bombshell in the Glamour Capital, 1928–1937*, Angel City Press, 2011.)

Fat chance. Not only is there an incomplete list of his films on the Internet Movie Database—with a brief and irrelevant biographical note—but one can view an entire feature-length film from 1932 called *Twisted Rails* on YouTube, starring Donovan. Elsewhere on the vast Web, a man named Steve Vaught has contributed a six-part history of Jack's house designing and building exploits, including accompanying run-ins with the law and scandals involving tenants, and innumerable references to movies and movie stars.

The reason I allude to these proofs of the man's existence is that I once wrote a brief item about Donovan in *The Globe and Mail*, and some readers thought I'd made him up, despite the fact that I published his mug shot from when, at the age of seventy-five, he was arrested for allegedly operating a stolen bicycle ring in Santa Barbara, California.

It was in Santa Barbara that I met him, in 1976 or '77. I hadn't been back in the United States since emigrating to Canada in '68. After eight or nine years, I was curious to have a look and, anyway, an Ontario winter was settling in.

I landed in Santa Barbara and, needing work, went to the California State Employment Agency and cited my experience as a gardener and landscaper. They sent me out for a job with "an old-time movie actor," who turned out to be Duncan Reynaldo, the man best known for playing the Cisco Kid on television. A nice man. He'd fix me a drink after I put in my hours on his beautiful grounds. I couldn't guess his nationality, and he told me that he couldn't either. His first memory was of being on a boat somewhere on the Mediterranean with people he found out were not his parents, nor his step-parents, or any other kind of relatives; he never figured out who they were. He grew up in an orphanage. But that's another story.

When that job was done, the man at the employment agency said, "Well, you got good reviews from the old actor and didn't bug him about putting in a word for you at the studios, so we're sending you to another old actor to paint the inside of his home. It's on Torremelinos Drive."

As I reached the address, a spry but elderly man with coppery face and hands, and white fluffs of hair jutting out from the sides of his yachting cap, wearing white slacks and holding a four-foot-high statue of the Virgin Mary in one hand, and an American flag on a pole in the other, was stepping off the porch. From behind the leaves of a century plant, I watched him start down the twisting flagstone walkway in a sort of energetic stagger. He stuck the flag-pole into a pile of stones, and set the Virgin on an ornate pedestal, turning it this way and that to get it just right.

With no warning, he turned abruptly to face me (or the century plant). "Roy, is that you behind that century plant? Why did you break into my house last night? Come out from behind there."

I did so, saying, "I'm not Roy. I'm Jim, and I was sent to paint your house."

At that moment, another character jumped down from the porch and came bounding across the parched zoysia grass. He was bald and missing most of his teeth; he looked like he'd just escaped from a chain gang in 1910. "Stay away from that one," he said to me, "or you'll just get in trouble." He then got into a Datsun pick-up truck and pulled away.

The man in the yachting cap looked after him and shook his head. "Looks like Erich von Stroheim's uglier brother."

"Or like he should be wading through the swamps with chains hanging from him in a Paul Muni prison movie, hound dogs barking in the background," I replied.

The man looked at me in a curious way, his white eyebrows raised, then nodded his head. He stepped forward and extended a tanned hand. "I'm Jack Donovan. Come on in the house, kid."

The inside of the ranch house looked like it held the contents of several antique shops and Goodwill stores, the furnishings of at least one old-time Hollywood restaurant, an art gallery, and the offices of a pair of mad scholars.

"I'm a cousin of Wild Bill Donovan. My mother married a man who owned *The St Louis Post-Dispatch*. I sneaked out of the house one day and rode a freight train to Hollywood when I was fourteen. When the old coot died, my mother joined me and I built a mansion for us in Santa Monica. I sold it to Mae Murray. She wanted me with it, but I was going with Clara Bow, see, the redhead, and on the side fooling around with Williams S. Hart's daughter. I wouldn't marry Mae, so for revenge she sued me. She loved suing people. I sued her back and soon I was addicted to suing people and it got me in a lot of trouble."

Jack showed me to a room crammed with two desks, on top of which were four typewriters, vials of pills, and four or five alarm clocks; two swivel chairs; piles of files on hardback chairs; and a heap of scrapbooks in one corner. Framed photographs took up much of the wall space.

As I stood on the threshold taking it in, he said, "People are trying to take advantage of me. I'm eighty years old, see, and—"

"Eighty!?"

I wasn't being polite to an old guy; I was truly surprised. He looked like a vigorous sixty-five-year-old California health nut.

"Yeah, eighty. And they think I'm ripe for the picking. They want to put me in a home, take away this house of mine. I'll sue them. They already took away my daughter."

"How could they take away your daughter?" I figured any daughter of his was probably middle-aged, or maybe she was handicapped and he had been taking care of her.

"She's eight years old and—"

"Eight! But you're—"

"Eighty. Heh, heh." His blue eyes twinkled. "Anyway, things are so bad that just a few years ago I got arrested for bicycle theft. They said I had a ring of kids stealing bikes for me and I'd resell them. They rousted me and took me to jail, kept me there for an entire month. Not only that, they knocked me around and—the indignity of it—cut my flowing locks before they took my mug shot. I got it here somewhere, I'll show you."

"Did you do it?"

He grinned and his eyes sparkled. "Now what kind of question is that?"

I stepped forward into the room to look at one of the photos on the wall. There was a platinum-blond woman in the arms of a young man who was smiling broadly in a white suit. "That's Jean Harlow. Who's the guy?"

"That's me, kid."

"What, were you some kind of actor?"

"Some kind. I was in dozens of pictures. First I played rah-rah college boys and young heroes, then I was a cowboy and a gangster."

I moved on to the next photograph: two smiling men, both in white suits; the older man had his hair parted in the middle; the younger man seemed like he hadn't a care in the world, and was too filled with energy to stay within the frame. "That you?"

"Yes, that's me."

I peered at the inscription. I could make out "Best of" and part of a signature: "Burroughs." It wasn't William S.

"The other man is Edgar Rice Burroughs. Ever heard of him?"

"Sure, the pulp writer. Came up with Tarzan."

"Burroughs, he was all right. I was making the serials and he came out to the lot one day. He knew I was an architect and wanted me to help with this development—Tarzana—he had a mind to build. It's now a town."

"Gee, you were an architect, too."

"Un-huh. Built half the mansions in Santa Monica. The yacht club, Canary Cottage, all sorts of joints. I was the first person in America to install what would come to be called French windows. But none of that matters, see. I have a son in prison on a bum rap. We got to go down to Chino and get him out. Will you help me, kid? I can size up a person right away, and I can tell you're on the level and not about to wilt under pressure. And that's all I need to know. Will you help me?"

"Sure thing, but what about painting your house?"

"Why do you want to paint my house?"

"Well, at the agency they said—"

"You don't have time to do that. This is Thursday morning, and I have to be in court on Monday. You'll be my witness. We have to prepare. First thing I want you to do is get on the phone and call Merv Griffin. I got to get on and tell the world about these corrupt judges down here. One time, years ago, one of them actually had me banned from making an appearance in the town of Santa Monica. I was not allowed within the city limits, wherever they are. Can you beat that?"

And so began a whirlwind association with Wild Bill's cousin Jack, who at eighty years old (at least) had more energy than just about any other three people I'd ever met. I served a four-month stint as chauffeur, hired con man, and confidant. We became an accustomed sight on the freeways of southern California in his battered baby-blue 1960 Cadillac convertible, back seat full of briefcases and paper bags filled with such essential items as dried figs, goat's milk, and apricots. A gym bag held blank paper, make-up, various eye glasses with different coloured frames, as well as a wig or two. The contents of the gym bag were for my use.

We also became an accustomed sight in various small-claims courts in the same area.

We bugged them at the *Los Angeles Daily Journal*, *The Los Angeles Times*, the executive offices of Standard Oil, and several smaller concerns. We made up fake ID and letters of reference; I worked for *Esquire*, a couple of Canadian newspapers (including *The Toronto Telegram*, which is no longer in existence), a Vancouver private investigation company called Fact Finders (which was in existence), and a few others. I used makeup pencils to thicken my eyebrows and darken the moustache that needed to be cultivated, but I drew the line at the wigs, mainly because I would have to cut my hair to get them to set properly—also they looked ridiculous.

Once, when we were rolling along Hollywood Boulevard, Jack said, "This was just a dirt path when I first came out here."

Jack got his first work in pictures after he was mustered out of the Army Air Corps after World War I, about which he rarely spoke. He flew planes in his first movies and played what were then known as "juvenile leads," though now the parts would be considered adult. At one point, a film magazine voted him the most promising actor of the year; the most promising actress was Joan Crawford. Jack worked in D.W. Griffith's pictures, and for DeMille, Chaplin, Raoul Walsh, Mack Sennett, and many others.

But all the time he was appearing in pictures, and later producing his own, he was a practising architect, building homes and restaurants and hotels, designing landscapes and even a life-saving system that was still in use on Southern California beaches when I knew Jack.

A Santa Monica newspaper described him in 1921 as "a dynamo of energy, an example to youth, a modern-day Renaissance man." *The Los Angeles Times* called him "the new Douglas Fairbanks."

But the great years weren't many in number. He started his fight with Mae Murray, and that lasted for years, leading to other imbroglios, and he no longer had much time to devote to movies and architecture. The cowboy films were just a means to pay his legal debts. The leading roles were followed by bit parts, which were followed by one-liners and walk-ons: He was the cop who squats down to examine the body in the alley; he was the bus driver who pulls the lever to open the doors. His last speaking part was in *The Untouchables*. The last role in which he appeared had him driving a hot rod in a beach-blanket movie in the early sixties, when he was seventy years old.

We'd be driving around and I'd be half listening to paranoid stories of his legal woes, hoping that his mind would take a detour and get back to Pola Negri, Rex Ingram, William Farnum, or Sally Eilers.

Once, rolling along, top down, on the San Bernardino Freeway, Jack said, apropos of nothing in particular, "You know that dame you hang around with? The one that I bet does peculiar things with those damn cougars? She wears all that paint and all those bracelets. That thing around her ankle. She reminds me of Lila Damita, Errol Flynn's first wife. One night she calls me up and says, 'Shack! Shack! You gotta comb help me. I need a plan. I muss have zat man Fleen. I muss. Come over now, Shack.' So I go over there and wind up staying all night doing my best to help her figure out a method of capturing 'Fleen.' I did my best till nearly noon the next day."

I only saw Jack appear depressed on two occasions. One was the day I drove him to the penitentiary in Chino where his son was incarcerated. He was moping as he crossed the parking lot to the Caddy after he'd been in there. "Sad, sad," he said. "That poor boy."

The other time was worse. I had asked if he had other children.

I knew about the eight-year-old daughter, but he told me he'd had another daughter who drowned when she was two years old and it was his fault, really. He and his wife Suzanne (Jack, at age fifty-one, finally ceased to be one of Southern California's most eligible bachelors when he married the twenty-two-year-old in 1945) had turned their attention away from the little girl and she took the opportunity to jump into the backyard wading pool. By the time Jack got there she was dead. The newspaper carried a picture of Jack with his head in his hands, weeping, the girl at his feet.

Oh, but he had great stories on all those other days, and we got up to all sorts of mischief. He had a crush on a young television reporter with the Santa Barbara station. No matter that she was fifty years younger than he. We used to drive up there, him in a sharp suit but still wearing the yachting cap, and both of us would approach her. He was hoping perhaps that I would blaze a trail for him. It didn't work out.

One time he was watching television while I leafed through a scrapbook and I heard him say, "Lord in heaven, look at that dame." It was Toni Tennille, who was singing while her husband played the piano. "I got to have the dame!"

"Maybe she'll dig you, Jack. You have a hat just like her husband's."

"Look at her bare back, would you?"

He gave me the assignment of getting in touch with Toni Tennille and pleading his case. The strange thing is, I did get in touch with her by phone, and convinced her to ease my life by just talking to him. I told her that he had once been a famous actor.

She consented to talk to Jack and at first she simply humoured him, but within a few minutes they were chatting amiably. I know because he had me listen in on the extension. I was disappointed when she told him she couldn't go out on a date with him because she was faithful to her husband. For a brief moment, I envisioned chauffeuring the two of them around in the convertible.

I hung around with Jack because I liked him and I liked his stories. He said, "You should have been with me in the old days, kid. You would have liked it. I needed a pal like you."

When they took away his visiting rights with his daughter—I

never did figure out who the mother was, or whether she really was his daughter—Jack grew despondent. He was running out of money, too, and I was near broke. I had to return to Canada. One night I called him from a pay phone out front of a bar restaurant that had an image of Humphrey Bogart from *The Treasure of the Sierra Madre* on its sign. The place was called The Fred C. Dobbs. I told him I was leaving.

"You can't do that, kid! I need you. Look, we'll sue these guys and then you can help me with this new design I drew up for a house in the hills, and you can be my campaign manager as I attempt for the third time to be mayor of Santa Barbara. Look, I'll call some people I know in Hollywood and we'll make a picture." His voice cracked, and I heard a sniffle. "What do you say to that, kid?"

"You're conning me, Jack."

There was a pause. "A little bit, kid. But just a little bit."

"Bye, Jack."

"Yeah, it's been fun. See you around, kid."

Edward John Trelawny
1792–1881

"Give me a for instance," I said many years ago to *NUVO*'s then managing editor, Lyndon Grove, when he proposed the idea of a column in the magazine about extravagant personages.

"For instance, Lord Byron," he said, and I replied, "Oh, I can give you more extravagant than that. How about his friend Trelawny?"

"Who?"

I knew Trelawny was a scalawag to the nth degree, but I also knew he had a reputation for being a liar, and no more than a hanger-on of the circle of Romantics that revolved around the poets Byron and Shelley in the early 1800s. He certainly needed more investigating, that I have now done. How much is true, and why did numerous chroniclers hate him so?

Edward John Trelawny was born in 1792 in London to Cornish parents so cruel and abusive that he was relieved at age twelve to be given over to the Royal Navy, to sail in the hold of an odiferous broken-down frigate, and be bossed by uneducated brutes. He worked on various ships and sailed all over the world until deserting. In a billiards parlour in Bombay, Trelawny, armed with a sword, was about to kill an older sailor in a brawl when another man intervened, taking the blade and replacing it with a cue stick. Thus Trelawny only severely beat the man, rather than killed him. The tall, dark,

IMAGE: Trelawny by the English painter Joseph Severn.

and handsome stranger told Trelawny to flee at once, and wait for him at a certain brothel in Dungaree. Two days later the stranger showed up and introduced himself as De Ruyter, a privateer sailing under a French letter of marque. Trelawny would later claim to have spent the next seven years aligned with De Ruyter, who spoke six languages fluently, read philosophy, and could quote reams of poetry. Trelawny modelled himself on this man who knew people all over the world, and was involved in all sorts of intrigues. They sailed together mostly in the southern seas, attacking slavers and taking prizes, many of them British.

Trelawny married an Arab girl called Zela, whom he had met during a raid on a city of slave-owning pirates on Madagascar. A year later, Zela was poisoned by a rival for Trelawny's affections. During his time as a corsair, Trelawny was shot and knifed several times, and he killed several people (who, he would insist, needed killing).

One fabulous adventure followed another until Trelawny and De Ruyter fled before the impeding assault on Mauritius, their base of operations, by the English under Lord Minto. They sailed to Saint-Malo, where De Ruyter left with dispatches to deliver to Napoleon. Trelawny continued with a Guernsey smuggler; he soon learned that his hero, De Ruyter, had been killed in a battle at sea.

A decade of fabulous adventures had come to an end.

"Or so he said," his biographers write. They don't believe he did what he said he did, yet can declare: "For long intervals we do not know where he was living or what he was doing." People later remarked upon his many wounds, obviously inflicted by bullets or knives, but gave no credence to his stories about obtaining them.

Why was Trelawny so regarded (or disregarded)? The answer lies in what came next. He was introduced in early 1822 to Percy Bysshe Shelley, who introduced him to Lord Byron. The latter—the ultimate would-be romantic hero—took one look at Trelawny, listened to his tales of adventure, and must have wanted to run and hide. Byron had become famous for a poem about a dashing corsair, and hinted that the work was to some extent autobiographical. Then along comes Trelawny with his long, flowing hair, black moustaches, absurd athletic prowess, and a violent, scarred past—the very model for what Byron had written. Worse for the class-conscious Byron was that Trelawny came from the same class—the upper— but couldn't have cared less. What made it all the more frustrating was that Trelawny looked the part of the corsair, while Byron— flabby, pale, and hobbled (not by a club foot, but by severed Achilles' tendons)—did not.

The women of the circle, particularly Shelley's wife, Mary, née Godwin, author of a novel called *Frankenstein,* gushed over the newcomer: "He is extravagant ... a mystery I am endeavouring to unravel," she told her diary the night they met. "He has the rare merit of exciting my imagination."

They had been introduced by Captain Daniel Roberts, who later wrote of Trelawny, "He was one of the most extraordinary characters of the age."

When Shelley was killed in a boating accident several months later, it was Trelawny who handled all arrangements, and even built the pyre on the beach where the great poet's body was burned. When only Shelley's heart remained, Trelawny reached into the fire to seize it. That spontaneous gesture was to make him famous (or infamous).

Not long before Shelley's death, the Greek War of Independence broke out. Trelawny left for Greece in 1823, and Byron followed in a newly purchased ship that carried his furnishings, linen, silver-ware, and eight servants. Byron rented a house at Missolonghi. Trelawny, however, joined the fighting and soon became attached to the rebel leader, Odysseas Androutsos. Androutsos was considered the purest of the vying rebel warlords, uncontaminated by political ambition; Trelawny became his second-in-charge. After raids, they would repair to Androutsos's stronghold on the north side of Mount Parnassus. The men were so close that Trelawny married Androutsos's half sister, Tersitza.

When Androutsos was captured and imprisoned, Trelawny became the leader of the rebel faction. He was shot twice by British spies, but survived his wounds. While he lay wounded in the caves, Androutsos was murdered in custody. Another rebel leader allowed Trelawny to be carried down from Mount Parnassus and taken onboard a ship bound for Italy.

Trelawny's exploits in Greece are well documented because the independence movement was a popular cause in England. Thus, all his swashbuckling, mountain guerrilla fighting, heroic horseback charges, and romancing of dusky women in exotic locales can be shown to have actually happened. Most of it was witnessed, and much of it made the papers. "Greece was the only time" sniffed one biographer, "that Trelawny came close to living up to his romantic image of himself." A recent biographer, however, begs to differ, insisting a scared Trelawny actually "hid in a cave during the revolution."

In Florence, Trelawny rented a house for his young wife and their new child, whom he named Zela, after his previous wife. There he recuperated and wrote a semi-autobiographical book about his youthful exploits, *Adventures of a Younger Son*. It was published in 1831 and was a huge success, and has been called "one of the greatest adventure stories ever written."

Trelawny's wife Tersitza eventually left him and their child and returned to Greece. Zela, who had been attending boarding school, was put up for adoption.

In early 1833, Trelawny set out for America. There, in New York City, he met the famous English actress Fanny Kemble who was on tour with her father. They travelled together to Niagara Falls and into Canada. Trelawny was last seen that year on December 2nd in Charleston, South Carolina, where he paid £1,000 for a black male slave and sent him to Canada via the Underground Railroad (the receipt of purchase still exists). This was not the first time he had bought and freed slaves. He'd done it throughout Asia and in Greece.

Then he disappeared. "For the first ten months of 1834, we do not know where he was or what he was doing," wrote one author, who was compelled to add: "Stories that he crossed the continent to California cannot be true."

Trelawny reappeared in Philadelphia in December, 1834, and left for England, "with a red Indian girl picked up somewhere on his travels."

The following year he married for the third time, to one Augusta Goring, and for twelve years lived peacefully in the country, building stone walls and planting flowers and trees. It is rumoured that he conducted affairs with many village women. During those years of domesticity, he began to write a book about his relations with Shelley and Byron and that circle—*Recollections of the Last Days of Shelley and Byron*, eventually published in 1858, and later revised and expanded as *Records of Shelley, Byron, and the Author* (1878)—which only incurred the enmity of the literati and added to his notoriety.

On visits to his club in London—appropriately named The Savage —awestruck visitors lined up to shake the hand of the man who had helmed Byron's ship, held the heart of Shelley in his hands, and battled heroically as a corsair for freedom in Greece.

Trelawny was much sought after as a guest at certain dinner parties—but not those of the conservative intelligentsia—where he yarned about eating human flesh, walking across the desert dressed as an Arab sheik, and knowing of buried treasure. He hit it off with the American poet Joaquin Miller, the "Bard of the Sierras," taking him aside to reveal the location of a shipload of gold buried near San Diego harbour.

Trelawny was sixty-five when his third marriage broke up and, after two months spent driving around the coast of England in his carriage, retired to a cottage in Sussex, where he became notorious among locals for his eccentricities. He painted his cottage red, wore no overcoat, nor socks, and could be seen in his eighties chopping wood outdoors in the winter. He tended his garden and maintained a bird sanctuary. He ate no meat and drank no alcohol. He frequently gave his possessions away to strangers. He received visitors to whom he retold his stories, promoted revolution, and argued for equal rights for women.

He sat for Sir John Everett Millais as the model for the old sea captain in his painting *The Northwest Passage* (1878). After seeing the painting for the first time, Trelawny went to Millais's house to challenge him to a duel.

Algernon Swinburne, the poet, came to see Trelawny and declared, "There is some fresh air in England yet while such an Englishman is alive." In his eighty-first year, Trelawny was "a magnificent old Viking to look at."

Strangers also showed up to his cottage. He wouldn't let them in, but they were content to stare at him from the other side of the fence as he chopped wood, for he was indeed a legend.

His best friends were a pair of dogs. He went every day to the village pond to feed the ducks. In 1881, Trelawny, one of the last great figures of the Romantic era, died in his sleep at age eighty-eight.

Herbert Dyce Murphy
1879–1971

Herbert Dyce Murphy never conned a greedy sucker out of his life savings, or convinced the natives of tropical isles that he was the returned white God of their myths. The man didn't even smoke or drink; yet, in the roster of scalawags, he has to be near the top. He was a mystery wrapped inside an enigma, hidden in a mass of contradictions somewhere in the land of the unfathomable.

Imagine a yacht being thrown about on a wild sea one dark night on the Mediterranean in 1902. The lone passenger wakes to

IMAGE: Herbert D. Murphy, photo by John George Hunter. Photo provided by the collections of the State Library of NSW.

discover that the entire crew lies paralyzed in a drunken stupor. The passenger rushes on deck to rescue the ship from disaster. "I never got such a fright in my life," Murphy would later say. Not due to any danger from the sea, but because he was in a soaked, transparent negligee, and certainly didn't want to be seen that way. But he was no ordinary transvestite; he was, in fact, a spy for British Military Intelligence posing as a woman.

Born in Australia in 1879, Murphy divided much of his youth between a mansion in Melbourne, the family sheep station spread over thousands of acres in Queensland and New South Wales, and London, where he served as a sort of *aide-de-camp* to Empress Eugénie, widow of Napoleon III and a distant relative.

It was obvious early on that he would not be the rugged Aussie He-Man his father had hoped for; nor did the boy want any part of such a life. At fourteen he sailed from England to the Norwegian Arctic. He would ship out at every break during his years at Tonbridge, a boarding school in Kent. In his spare time, he studied photography and taught himself to print and develop pictures. He spent his entire sixteenth year working aboard a wool clipper. The following year, he went on his first Arctic whaler and seemed always to be doing something heroic: rescuing people, or taking over the ship when the captain was incapacitated. He became a second mate after only four years at sea.

Later, Murphy enrolled at Oxford, but left to sign on to a ship bound for the Gulf of Mexico because he would get leave in New Orleans, which boasted a brand new railroad line. Murphy was crazy for trains.

Back at Oxford, he tried out for the school play and earned the eponymous lead female role in Euripides' *Alcestis*. "None of the young ladies who auditioned," he recalled, "could recite the Greek."

As fortune would have it, the master of the college took as his guest to the play the director of British Military Intelligence, Sir John Ardagh. "Alcestis is a beautiful girl," Ardagh said. "Who is she?" When told the truth, Ardagh shook his head in wonder. "I suppose he's quite effeminate?"

"Quite the contrary," answered the master.

Within a couple of days, Herbert, or Dyce, as he was known, ceased to be a student and became a spy.

British Military Intelligence, fearing war with France, wanted extensive information about the state of railways on the continent, and had been trying to gather it for over a year. Two agents had been discovered and sent home. Ardagh surmised that a "woman" might do the job undetected. Not only could Murphy look the part, his interest in trains and ability as a photographer made him ideal.

After a month of tutoring by a female crew, he emerged as Australian heiress Edith Murphy. Soon he was travelling in France and Belgium. During these trips he was often accompanied by an elderly sea captain. A painting exists of the two of them in a railway carriage. (But it was another painting that would help make Murphy infamous: E. Phillips Fox's *The Arbour*, in which Murphy is supposedly the girl in the white dress. Many who knew Murphy well deny it—not that they don't believe he's in the painting, but rather insist he is actually the woman in the *striped* dress.)

On Christmas day, 1901, while in London, Murphy and two friends from Military Intelligence decided at the last moment to go to church. Murphy's family had a pew in Holy Trinity and, assuming his mother to be away in Australia, went there with his friends. But indeed his mother was in London, and she showed up at the church. She failed to recognize her son, and was extremely put out to see strangers in the Murphy pew. Murphy passed her a note: "I'm your daughter, Edith." His mother replied with her own note: "I am so glad. I always wanted a beautiful daughter."

This incident, and the Fox painting, later inspired a novel by the Australian Nobel laureate Patrick White, *The Twyborn Affair*, short-listed for the Booker Prize.

King George VII took quite a fancy to "Edith," and there supposedly exists a photograph of the two together.

Rudyard Kipling was introduced to him and later said, "I frankly do not believe that was a man."

But Murphy was getting older, his skin coarser, and dark hairs were appearing on the backs of his hands. And he was becoming notorious. Finally, he'd had enough. After two months in seclusion on the Canary Islands, he shipped out as second mate on a whaler to Antarctica. On another whaler, in the South Pacific, Murphy got in trouble with the skipper for trying to smuggle several naked island women aboard the ship.

In the north of Norway, Murphy unofficially adopted two little girls, aged four and six—the sole survivors of an avalanche that had wiped out their town—after the local pastor had begged him to take them. They would stay with him for twelve years, accompanying him on numerous trips.

In 1911, he was one of only twenty-eight men accepted for the Australasian Antarctic Expedition, led by Sir Douglas Mawson. (Murphy had volunteered for Ernest Shackleton's 1908 Antarctic expedition, but was turned down, supposedly for being too effeminate—a charge he denied.) The expedition was gone for sixteen months. The two orphan girls had been put in boarding school in Tasmania. The surviving journals of the expedition crew members all mention Murphy keeping them in stitches with stories of his adventures and misadventures.

After the expedition, and after he was jilted by the woman with whom he was in love, Murphy spent many years sailing around the world for a whaling company, checking on supplies, and establishing depots.

Back in Australia in the 1920s, Murphy bought sixteen hectares of land along the beach in Mount Martha, a suburb of Melbourne, and opened his property to children and their parents. There was never the slightest hint of any impropriety in his friendships with children, nor with anyone else. Over the years he supported the education of several needy children. And later, there were four young women whom he supported all the way through medical school.

He devoted much of his later life to giving talks at various clubs and societies, for which he accepted no payment. Of course, as with so many who live outsized lives, Murphy's stories have constantly been dismissed. Even those who liked him, smirked knowingly where his adventures are concerned. "Yes, he was a wonderful raconteur but you couldn't believe a word he said." Trouble is none of these people, including biographers, can explain why his stories were not true. One biographer barely mentions the fifteen years Murphy spent providing a holiday home to children, and never contacted, or simply disregarded the reminiscences of, these people. Some insist that after the 1920s Murphy never travelled at all, "except for an annual cruise to the Norwegian Arctic"! Yet one girl recalls how during the Depression, he took her and her mother on board his yacht and they sailed to Ceylon and back.

In 1934, when he was fifty-four, Murphy married Muriel Idrene Nevile Webster at St. John's Church in Toorak.

Murphy used to say that during winters when he was in his sixties, he would ship to the Arctic. One doubter claims that records show he was actually in attendance at Melbourne City Council meetings during these times. But they don't, in fact, show that he was in attendance *every* winter, nor is there any record of him being anywhere else when he wasn't in attendance. Where was he?

Wherever he lived, Murphy built a small trolley-railway on his property. He'd drive the locomotive, and fill the gondolas with garden clippings, or give children rides. He was thus occupied one day in 1952 when his wife summoned him to the telephone. It was a ship's captain named Ericson; two days later, Murphy was a mate on *The Tottan*, bound for Adélie Land to relieve the beleaguered French Antarctic Expedition. He was seventy-three years old. Yet Murphy never mentioned this incident to anyone but his wife. It would have caused embarrassment for the captain and the French.

Murphy lived to be ninety-one years old, and in his last few years could be seen walking or riding his bike around Melbourne. One girl, who had been at his estate during holidays, was visiting her mother in the late 1960s when she saw Murphy walking down the street with his hands held in front of him in handcuffs. She brought him inside and helped the old man get out of the cuffs, and served him tea.

He passed away in July, 1971.

Charles Laseron, a biologist on Mawson's Antarctic expedition, declared "Herbert is a genius...his stories are convincing yet at the same time too impossible to be true." Laseron didn't say why.

Murphy's wife burned many of his papers and journals—

including, supposedly, proof of a previous marriage—in 1917. Among the material that survived are photographs that he'd taken of women in all parts of the world. There are, as well, the King's and the Queen's South Africa Medals for meritorious service in the Boer War. No one who knew him remembered Murphy ever mentioning that country!

Suzanne Valadon
1865–1938

Suzanne Valadon is forever associated with the streets of Montmartre, from the days of the Paris Commune in 1871, to far beyond her death in 1938.

She was born in Bessines-sur-Gartempe in 1865 as Marie-Clémentine Valadon; her birth certificate listed her mother as a maid, and her father as "unknown."

When she was four, her stepfather, a small-time crook, was busted for counterfeiting and sent to the penal colonies in French Guinea, after which mother and daughter relocated to Montmartre. The area had only recently become part of the city of Paris, and barns and farmhouses shared the top of the hill with cafés, studios,

IMAGE: Madame Suzanne Valadon, born in Montmarte, returned there to become famous as a painter. Photo ca. 1926. Copyright Bettman/CORBIS. Used under license.

and dancehalls with sawdust floors. Artists had flocked to Montmartre because of the cheap prices and great views of the city. Two-bit circuses performed in the squares; painters set up their easels on the corners and worked alongside buskers. Théophile Gautier called it "the opera of the streets."

Young Marie was a wild tomboy, usually in trouble. At age seven she began to draw using charcoal fallen from coal wagons; the sidewalks were her sketchpads. To attract attention, and in hopes of making a few centimes, she took to hanging around Père Lachaise Cemetery on days when there were funerals. She would summon up her best woebegone expression and sometimes break into tears, and this occasionally resulted in a few coins from mourners who thought she might be somehow connected to the departed.

Her mother, who supported them by taking in sewing, put the girl in a convent school hoping to tame her. It didn't work. Marie fell in love with the poetry and life of François Villon. When she was ten years old, Marie was taken out of the convent and sent to work decorating women's hats; later she waited on tables, sold vegetables at Les Halles market, made wreaths in a factory—but all the time she was drawing. Later she recalled that "at age eight I wanted to grasp and hold the trees and their limbs so that I could keep them forever."

One of her pleasures was to climb things, be they trees or buildings. Neighbours summoned the fire trucks once when Marie was spotted six storeys up an apartment building swinging from a French window.

She liked to follow behind parades, doing flips and turning cartwheels; sometimes she did handstands on the horses' backs. Her antics attracted the attention of the circus owner Ernest Molier, who trained her to be a performer. While learning the trapeze, she appeared in pantomimes and danced nude in front of men. By the time she was a teenager, Marie was a full-fledged trapeze artist and would probably have remained with the circus, but after a year she suffered a bad fall that ended her career. (Years later, when asked how she survived her tough early life, she merely shrugged, "In order to achieve greatness one must take the hard knocks.")

While recuperating, she decided to devote her life to art, a seemingly impossible dream for a working-class female in 1880. There were few female painters at the time, and all of them were from the upper-middle class who had the money for lessons and leisure to pursue their hobby. Marie had no money for art classes, and no women to look up to. She had only her will. Of course a mere glance at a photograph of her as a young, or even middle-aged woman, indicates she had something else to offer: a beautiful face, and a curvaceous figure but, unlike many other adventuresome female scalawags, she did not use these attributes to get by, although she certainly used them for enjoyment.

A friend who was a model took her around to artists' studios and Valadon, now fifteen and calling herself Maria, joined the other girls on Sundays at a sort of unofficial models market in Place Pigalle. There, she attracted the attention of the very popular painter Pierre-Cécile Puvis du Chavannes, and began to model for him, as she soon would for Pierre-Auguste Renoir, Edgar Degas, Henride Toulous-Lautrec, Amedeo Modigliani, and many lesser-known artists. She was short and curvy, and had what one commentator called "luminous blue eyes that attracted men like flies."

She was a regular at the notorious bistros of the day, such as Le Lapin Agile, which is still around. There was also Le Chat Noir, where the bourgeoisie was not welcome. There was a riot one night when several pimps tried to take over the place and kidnap some of the girls, including Valadon, who was there that night. There were knives and guns, and Valadon escaped via the rooftop.

In December, 1883, she gave birth to a son and, as on her own birth certificate, the father is listed as "unknown." There has been endless speculation over the matter of paternity. The most frequently named candidates consist of several art students, the postman, and Renoir and Degas, for whom she had been modelling for at least a year before the boy was born. A joke about the child's parentage was soon making the rounds of Montmartre: After the child's birth, Valadon took him to Renoir, who said, "It can't be mine, the colour is terrible." Next she visited Degas: "He can't be mine, the form is terrible." Then she ran into a young painter named Miguel

Utrillo, and told him her troubles. He replied, "I would be glad to put my name to the work of either Renoir or Degas."

After a few years, Utrillo legally adopted the boy, who grew up to be the famous painter and alcoholic Maurice Utrillo.

Valadon began painting in 1892, and Degas encouraged her efforts.

By now, having changed her name to Suzanne—Toulouse-Lautrec had nicknamed her "Suzanne" after the Biblical story of Susanna and the Elders—the tempestuous artist got involved with the young composer Erik Satie, who was devastated by her when they met, and devastated by her when she broke up with him six months later, during which time he wrote her three hundred letters. He was extremely jealous, particularly of her penchant for appearing in nightclubs wearing nothing but a mask. Satie wrote his famous piece "Vexations" after his short, but intense, relationship with Valadon, and was never to have another love affair.

During all these liasons, Valadon kept working and caring for her son Maurice, an awkward and unhappy boy. She could not afford to pay models for her portrait painting, so time and again she painted Maurice and her own mother. Then, after a life of poverty, Valadon, at the age of thirty-one, suddenly married a wealthy stockbroker named Paul Mousis in 1896. Her friends didn't understand, but Mousis was a solid, manly man, a relief from wishy-washy artists, and she thought that now without financial worries, with homes in the city and country, she could get a lot of painting done. Yet for nearly a decade she did almost no work; ironically, however, her career began to flourish due to Degas's support and the interest of the contemporary art dealer Ambroise Vollard.

One afternoon in 1906, her drunken son, Maurice, was brought home by another young man, the would-be painter André Utter. The friend and the mother fell in love on the spot. The fact that the man was twenty-one years younger did not matter at all. Valadon later wrote that meeting Utter meant "a renewal" of her life, and for the first time her passion was equal to that of the man. She threw over her homes and marriage (Mousis officially divorced Valadon in 1910) and resumed a bohemian life with Utter in Montmartre.

When Valadon's painting of herself and Utter, *Adam and Eve,* was shown, it marked the first time a painting of a naked man and a naked woman together was ever exhibited in public.

When Utter enlisted in the army at the outset of the First World War, the couple was married so that Valadon could get the wife's allowance. She became close friends with Amedeo Modigliani, about whom she was always discreet. For his part, Modigliani claimed, "She is the only woman who ever understood me."

Over the previous ten years, Valadon's son Maurice had become more of a drunk, and more successful, at least financially, with his painting. He was in and out of jail and asylums while his paintings flew off the walls. When the war ended, Utter, Valadon, and Maurice pooled their resources and bought a house together. Valadon also bought a Panhard touring car, fed sirloin to her dogs, and caviar to her cats. She was notorious for throwing huge picnics in the Paris Métro, spontaneously picking fifty children off the streets and taking them to the circus, and giving money to every *clochard* she encountered. This did not sit well with her new husband, who was upset by always having to bail Maurice out of jail, and with being the third most well-known painter in the family.

Valadon turned sixty in 1925, and Utter turned to other women. Once, upon discovering that her husband intended to take one of his girlfriends to their country home, Valadon followed and caught the couple in bed. She locked them in the room and kept them there for a week. For food, they had to lower a bucket down from their window. Valadon filled it with boiled cabbage.

Valadon's habits became more and more eccentric, her exploits more and more antic. When she was young and beautiful, her activities were considered titillating, but in the later years, people found her embarrassing. She clothed herself in rags, walked around in huge moccasins, smoked a pipe, and flirted with everything in pants. But at age seventy she found a new man, a Russian half her age who painted and played the guitar. He was called Gazi, and he did her shopping, cooked her meals, and serenaded her with songs that he wrote. When the romance was but a year old, Valadon was hospitalized with diabetes.

In 1938, a couple of weeks before she died, Valadon told her friend Francis Carco, a chronicler of Montmartre, that her satisfaction lay in the fact that "I have never surrendered. I have never betrayed anything I believed in."

She died at her easel on April 7. The newspaper *Le Figaro* announced "the death of the wife of painter André Utter and mother of Maurice Utrillo."

Should one want to tour the streets of Montmartre where Valadon walked, one might start out at the bottom of the hill at Place Suzanne-Valadon. The house where she lived much of her life, on rue Cortot, is now the Musée de Montmartre.

There is even an asteroid named for her: 6937 Valadon. This is entirely fitting, because she was her own bright, small planet, and in no one else's orbit.

William Leonard Hunt
1838–1929

In 1859, at the foot of Walton Street in Port Hope, Ontario, a local boy named William Leonard Hunt walked a tightrope over the Ganaraska River. He had been offered one hundred dollars to do it, but he demanded five hundred, promising to stand on his head above the river. Hunt kept his promise, as well as doing somersaults and walking blindfolded without a balancing pole. Just a few months later, he was calling himself Signor Guillermo Antonio Farini, after an obscure Italian revolutionary, and in 1860 became the second man in history to cross Niagara Falls on a tightrope. The Ganaraska walk marked the public beginning of a long, strange life—a life so full of adventure, tragedy, achievement, and mystery that it might give pause to the gullible. But pause is one of the few things the Great Farini never did.

IMAGE: "The Great Farini with his protégé, Lulu (left)." Photo by Ron Roels, © The Niagara Falls (Ontario) Public Library.

I first heard of him from Daniel P. Mannix, historian and ex-sideshow performer. For many years, Mannix had been a world champion sword swallower, and he knew everything about sideshows and "freaks" (not a pejorative). Mannix described Farini as a former rope-walker and acrobat who had performed amazing acts in venues around the world, and called him a "mysterious figure with a dark past."

He didn't know the half of it.

William Hunt was born in June, 1838, in Lockport, New York, and grew up in Southern Ontario near Port Hope. At an early age, Willie became entranced by the circus and yearned to be a performer. To this end, he began a regimen of exercise and acrobatics. He worked out with weight scales and climbed the sides of the family barn using pegs he'd drilled into the walls. Soon he was showing off at town fairs. One morning, he strung a rope from a stake in the ground to the loft of a barn and walked all the way on his third attempt. A couple of months later, Willie was walking across the Ganaraska.

As the Great Farini, he joined the famous Dan Rice circus—Rice was the clown who became a confidant of President Lincoln, and was in fact the man upon whom Uncle Sam is modelled—but quit to roam the Wild West, where he got into all sorts of scrapes. In the summer of 1860, he was at Niagara Falls to challenge the Great Blondin, the first man to cross the falls on a rope.

Farini successfully completed not only that first walk, but also many others over the summer. His goal seemed not only to outdo Blondin, but to test the limits of daring. Blondin's act was based on making it all appear effortless; Farini drew crowds with the allure of disaster. On his first crossing, Farini lowered himself from the midpoint to the deck of the Maid of the Mist, drank a glass of wine, and then climbed back up to the tightrope above. After making it to the other side, he returned blindfolded and wearing baskets on his feet.

"It can't be done!" was the usual comment before each of his subsequent exploits. Over the next few weeks, Farini hung upside-down over the raging tumult, gripping the rope with his toes; he cooked an omelette over a stove in the middle of the walk; he carried a washtub and washed handkerchiefs using water he collected in a bucket from the river below; and performed other acrobatic feats.

Later, a crowd of fifteen thousand saw him walk along a wire strung thirty-seven metres above the Chaudière Falls near Ottawa. According to Shane Peacock, author of a marvellous biography of the man, whenever Farini was mentioned the hottest topic was how he was going to die.

Farini toured the world and, along with the tightrope walking, gave exhibitions of strength and gymnastics. He was also a gifted mechanic, and from his youth had been interested in creating new gadgets and machinery.

Newspaper reporters often made mention of the number of females in the audiences of the handsome and well-muscled Farini. There were rumours of several marriages, and there *were* actual marriages during his youth, but these remain shrouded in mystery.

In 1862, Farini abruptly quit show business to join the Union Army in the War Between the States. He was employed by General George McClellan to devise quick and efficient ways of crossing creeks and rivers. McClellan later used Farini on intelligence missions. But when President Lincoln removed the general from command after the disastrous loss of life at the Battle of Antietam, Farini left the Union Army and went to Havana, Cuba, with his first verifiable wife, a Hope township girl named Mary Osbourne.

He had been training Mary to hold on to his back while he walked the tightrope. In Havana one afternoon, Farini accomplished four solo crossings of the Plaza del Toros in front of a crowd of thirty thousand. He then started a fifth crossing, carrying Mary. When they were almost at the end, Mary suddenly removed one arm from around her husband's neck to wave to the wildly cheering crowd. In tightrope walking, any spontaneous gesture can mean tragedy, and Mary fell. Then, in what may be the most incredible move in the entire history of tightrope walking, Farini caught his wife, clutching her dress with one hand. He lowered himself until he had hooked the backs of his knees over the rope. But before he could pull her up, the dress ripped and Mary fell to her death.

Incredibly, Farini was soon performing again. Having walked a tightrope over Niagara Falls several times already, Farini attempted in 1864 to cross the river above the falls on a pair of specially made stilts. (He failed when one of the stilts got caught in a crevice and broke, forcing him to be rescued from Robinson Island.)

He went back to the tightrope, but after a few shows, lonely and distraught, he disappeared into South America. After six months of wandering the continent, he emerged in Europe doing a wire and trapeze act. In the late 1860s, he began training and travelling with a ten-year-old boy whom he advertised as his son, or "El Niño." Where he found him—whether on the street, in an orphanage, or elsewhere —has never been determined.

After a couple of seasons, Farini began to train and manage other acrobats, and debuted what he declared was a sensational new female act: the glorious, high-flying Lulu, who soon became a sensation in Europe and the Americas. By all newspaper accounts, Lulu was beautiful, with long, wavy blond hair, and she garnered dozens of marriage proposals. But Lulu was actually El Niño in drag. As time went on and Lulu was no longer able to pass as a woman, he presented himself as Lu, doing his act in female trapeze artist garb, but with hair shorn and parted, and his moustache waxed.

By the time he reached his thirties, Farini's own career as a tightrope walker and trapeze artist was over; he feared he'd be seriously injured if he continued. He devoted himself to inventing and promoting new acts and roaming the world in search of human and animal oddities. He originated what became known as the human cannonball act. But perhaps his greatest sensation was Krao, advertised as the "Ape Woman" or "Darwin's Missing Link." The girl was completely covered in hair, with a mane flowing down her back, and was said to be a member of a race of tree dwelling, ape-like people. Farini claimed to have found her in Siam, and perhaps he did. Doctors and scientists examined Krao and admitted they didn't know what she was.

In 1885, Farini again quit show business, and with Lu (by now a bearded photographer) disappeared into southern Africa, where they spent several months exploring the Kalahari Desert. (Farini is allegedly the first white man to have ever survived crossing the desert on foot.) In his book about the region, published the following year, Farini claimed to have found the remains of a vanished civilization. Explorers have been looking for his Lost City of the Kalahari ever since.

The African trip just added to his legend. He was a man to whom legends attached. Still handsome and vigorous, and speaking seven languages, he had seemingly been everywhere and was as liable to be found in the company of a pinhead (a term for a microcephalic on the sideshow circuit) or tattooed lady, as with a baron or earl.

After returning to Europe, Farini continued to book circus and music hall acts. But by the late 1880s, he was spending most of his time on his inventions and a new enthusiasm: growing begonias. (He eventually wrote a book about the plants.) He also patented many inventions, including the modern parachute and folding theatre seat. Back in Canada in the late 1890s, Farini backed and co-invented, with Frederick Knapp, a huge roller boat that, it was claimed, would make the crossing to Europe in two days. On September 8, 1897, the day it was christened, it barely got out of Toronto Harbour and was eventually used as landfill for the new harbourfront in the late 1920s.

In his sixties, Farini took up painting. In 1911, he went to Europe with his German-born wife, Anna, and was caught in Germany when the First World War broke out. He spent his time painting, keeping a detailed diary, and translating war accounts from German publications.

After the war, Farini returned to Port Hope with Anna. They existed on his wife's small inheritance, and on the sales of parcels of Farini's land holdings. In his eighties, Farini was a familiar sight riding his bicycle on the streets of the small town and on dirt roads in the country. He would pedal ten kilometres to a relative's farm and pitch in with the chores. He is remembered vaulting onto wagons with the agility of an athletic teenager. The rest of his time was spent painting.

The brooding young man with an arrogant demeanour and a Svengali-like presence had mellowed into a kindly old artist and storyteller. Not that the older citizens believed his tales of duals and gunfights, of pygmies and lost cities, of the applause of thousands. Little kids did, however, and they followed him around town, calling "Freeny, Freeny!"

In 1929, at an age and in a manner that those early commentators would never have predicted, the Great Farini died in bed of influenza. He was ninety years old.

Nowadays in Port Hope, you can walk along the river that he crossed by rope 150 years ago, stop at a restaurant named after him, have a "Farini schnitzel," and raise a toast to the memory of the extravagant Great Farini.

Edward James
1907–1984

"You did not *know* Edward. He was a *happening* which you lived through, sometimes like a dream, often like a nightmare."
—A friend of James's

It was early one morning, on the terrace of the San Ignacio Hotel in Xilitla, Mexico, when I asked the manager where the strange buildings were. He pointed toward a line of mountains carpeted with dense, dark-green foliage, and reminiscent of the South Seas.

"That way," he said, shaking his head as if in wonderment at something he couldn't understand.

"What about the man who built them?" I asked.

He shook his head with the same expression.

I set out on a five-kilometre walk down a dirt road through a kind of paradise, at the sides of which grew wild *Impatiens* and marigolds. The air was scented by gardenias. I passed an old lady

IMAGE: The Edward James Foundation

bent like a question mark, and then was passed by two white horses ambling along like a couple of buddies taking the air and cutting up jackpots.

And then, rounding a bend, I saw twisting and poking their way up through the thick forest canopy twenty cement treetops, and a couple of strides later got a look at giant snakes, gates, clamshells, lotus blossoms, towers, and stairways to the stars.

This all came back to me the other evening as I watched an old movie, a weird psycho-sexual western from 1946 called *Duel in the Sun*. The female star is Jennifer Jones, a "half-breed" Mexican. The film opens with her mother dancing on top of the bar in a saloon in Mexico. She's all sensual fire, dark legs revealed through rustling skirts as she stomps her high-heeled shoes and tosses her thick black hair, her eyes flashing appropriately. After her dance, she goes off with the richest of her admirers.

The dancer was an Austrian star of European ballet and musicals named Tilly Losch. Jennifer Jones should have packed her bags and crossed the Rio Grande. She couldn't follow *that*. And Edward James was married to *that*.

Edward William Frank James was born in England in 1907 to parents who had each inherited tremendous fortunes. Their houses were always filled with kings and dukes. After the birth of his four sisters, Edward's father was rumoured to have become impotent, and that the Prince of Wales (later King Edward VII) was his real father. James denied this, insisting that Edward VII was only his grandfather. His father died when James was five. His domineering mother seemed dedicated to only two things in life: miserliness, and obsessively criticizing her son.

When James was sent off to Eton at thirteen, his mother gave him stern warnings about homosexuals. After some terrible years, he convinced his mother to let him go to Institut Le Rosey in Switzerland. There he displayed habits that would be noted throughout his life: he was always late; always forgetting things; always dreaming; and his laughter was a sort of high-pitched screech. Of James at eighteen, a tutor wrote, "He is so childish for his years and requires the same kind of handling as a small boy."

James's first sexual experiences were with girls. At Oxford, other boys made fun of his dreaminess and childlike nature. He spent his time writing poetry, taking flying lessons, and sending off twenty-page letters to his mother and the servants. After graduation, he went to New York City to stay with a half-cousin, Arthur Curtiss James, one of the wealthiest men in America. While there, James and a girlfriend stole a sandhill crane from the Bronx Zoo. The theft made the papers. It was a mystery: How did culprits snatch a bird that size, and where was it? Fortunately or unfortunately, cousin Arthur was on the zoo board. The crane was returned just as mysteriously as it had disappeared, but James was sent packing.

Back in Europe, James somehow got himself appointed honorary attaché to the British embassy in Rome. One has to wonder: *What* were they thinking? He spent most of his time ignoring his duties and entertaining lavishly. He once hosted a lobster dinner, and had the chef place working electric light bulbs in the eye sockets of the crustaceans.

James's job was the deciphering of cables, but he was in the habit of writing nasty letters on embassy stationery to strangers, one of them being Mussolini. James made a mistake with a cable, stating that Italy was building nine hundred thousand submarines, and for a couple of days Great Britain was on a war footing. When it was learned that the actual number was nine, James was again sent packing. He'd later say, "It's the only job I ever had."

In 1930, James saw Tilly Losch on stage and it was love (and lust) at first sight. He besieged her with gifts and poetry, and they were soon married. One day he watched as Tilly emerged from the shower and walked up the stairs dripping wet. He was entranced by her footprints on the wood of the stairways. He had casts made, and Tilly's footprints woven into a rug.

James and Tilly fought continuously, and their 1934 divorce was appropriately stormy. He sued, claiming she was having an affair with Prince Serge Obolensky. She countersued, claiming James was a homosexual (he was, in fact, bisexual), basing her suit on the fact that she had heard some Italian tenor singing with happiness in their home. In court, the tenor produced his passport to show that he was in Argentina at the time of the happy singing; James had been playing records.

Although James would soon fall in love again, with actress and model Ruth Ford, men would otherwise dominate his romantic life.

James devoted himself to being a patron of the arts, commissioning works from numerous singers, dancers, and painters. He was René Magritte's first patron, and for many years Salvador Dalí's main patron. In 1937, Magritte produced *The Pleasure Principle (Portrait of Edward James)*, and his most famous painting, for which James was the model: *La reproduction interdite*. The latter depicts from behind a man looking in a mirror, but the image in the mirror is the back of the man looking in the mirror.

James collaborated with Dalí on the famous *Dream of Venus* pavilion at the 1939 World's Fair in New York. As well, James hired Dalí to transform his Monkton Cottage in England, home to Dalí's notorious Mae West Lips Sofa, which James had commissioned. He also started a press to produce expensive hand-bound books with luxurious paper.

James eventually broke off relations with Dalí, repulsed at his greed and avarice, but the final rupture occurred when Dalí lent his support to General Franco, who would overthrow the democratic government of Spain and install a military dictatorship. The Republican loyalist forces at the time had one bomber plane, given to them by James.

When he wasn't handing out money, buying paintings and animals, or collaborating with artists, James was making friends and fighting with them, and travelling almost incessantly. Like the little child that he had been and was still in many ways, James would lose track of where he put his toys—be they houses, boa constrictors, books, or paintings. He was forever showing up at the airport without his passport. Once, intending to fly to Scotland, he wound up in Iceland. He liked the country so much, he kept returning.

His activities are impossible to trace. He once wrote a letter to a friend called Brink Jackson, apologizing for not meeting him in Paris as planned because Ruth Ford had refused his third marriage proposal, so he'd travelled to Romania to see a shepherd who had met Christ.

James bought and sold houses all over the world. Nevertheless, he would stay in hotels. At one point he was banned from the five best hotels in Los Angeles. One hotel manager refused him a room, saying, "The plumber's bill will be more than the room rent." (James was obsessive when it came to washing himself.)

James employed secretaries at each of his owned or rented domiciles. Some secretaries lasted for years, others minutes. One of the former was a Miss Prufrock, who was frequently to be seen beside James in the front seat of his Rolls-Royce or Duesenberg, taking dictation. One of the latter was Lauren Bacall's mother. The American poet Mary Barnard lasted two weeks. "I got the job," she said, "because I could spell Tchelitchew and Klee." She showed up for work one day at his hotel room in New York, only to find that he had gone, leaving behind "three shoes, four of his art works on the wall and his suspenders on the couch."

Most of the artists he knew played at surrealism; they either posed as surrealists, as did Dalí, or led conservative lives while turning out surrealist works of art, as did Magritte. James lived a genuinely surreal life, and had been doing so for a couple of decades, and then, in 1947, he found Xilitla.

James had been travelling around Mexico with a handsome young man he had met in Cuernavaca named Plutarco Gastélum. They were in the mountainous regions of San Luis Potosí when they came across a waterfall in the jungle. Decades later when I visited, Gastélum's son, Plutarcito, said to me, "My father and Mr. James went for a swim in the pool at the foot of the waterfall. After a couple of minutes, Mr. James realized their chests and shoulders were covered by butterflies. And he said to my father, 'This is it.'"

Xilitla (*Hee-leet-luh*) was not a town that tourism had forgotten; it had never shown up. James bought the land around the waterfall and immediately had the idea to raise orchids and provide a refuge for animals. But one morning, staring out over his property, James had a vision in which he saw the riotous vegetation that surround- ed him duplicated in a mirror-image jungle made of cement. It was like a vegetal dream that mirrored his own complex subconscious, and he immediately set to work, drawing up plans, and hiring dozens of local people to help bring his dream to fruition.

The work went on for years. In the meantime, Plutarco got married and James had a house—Posada El Castillo—built for him in town. James would continue to travel all over the world, but spent most of each year at his jungle paradise—his "Surrealist Xanadu"—which he called Las Pozas ("The Pools"). James spent over $5 million constructing Las Pozas, selling his collection of surrealist art at auction to pay for it.

He died in San Remo, Italy, in 1984.

James attracted detractors and sycophants all of his life; many of these were the same people. They liked to portray him as a failed artist with a big pocket book. Even Las Pozas, it has been said, was the work of Plutarco Gastélum, not James. This is ridiculous. In a cottage near the site, I discovered two trunks filled with sketches and drawings by James. The people who had possession of these trunks had taken care of Las Pozas after it had fallen into neglect. There were dozens of his drawings, and they served as working plans for the monuments and sculptures at the site.

One other thing of note: James had misshapen feet (his mother tried to save money when he was a boy by making him wear the same shoes for years). When he was putting up the house for Plutarco, James recalled the casts he had made of Tilly's footprints, and cast his own weirdly shaped feet in cement. From these he made a footpath to El Castillo. Stepping stones in the form of cement footprints are now ubiquitous; James would get a laugh—a high-pitched screech—out of this, knowing that all over the world people are literally following in his misshapen path.

Peters and Weinberg
1885–1959 & 1890–1960

A few years ago Steven Spielberg directed *Catch Me If You Can*, a movie about the famous imposter Frank Abagnale, Jr., played by Leonardo DiCaprio. Back in 1961, Tony Curtis portrayed a much more interesting scoundrel named Ferdinand Waldo Demara, Jr. in *The Great Impostor*. Neither of these men, however, matched the roguish achievements of Frederick Emerson Peters; and as for the audacious Stephen Jacob Weinberg, a.k.a. Stanley Clifford Weyman, or any of seven other names that we know of, well, that man from Brooklyn performed in his own league.

IMAGE: Photo courtesy of Library of Congress. LC–F8–15225.

Demara and Abagnale passed themselves off as doctors; Peters and Weinberg did that to fill time before they could put more daring scams in play. Abagnale posed as a pilot; Weyman got away with being a lieutenant commander in the French Navy. Reviewing the lives of Demara and Abagnale, one concludes that despite their troubled upbringings, or because of them, both men wished to be respectable citizens. That was not the case with Peters and Weinberg; they were born to be outrageous miscreants. And they were lovable, too.

Born into an upright family in Cleveland in 1885, Frederick Emerson Peters ran away from home at age sixteen and got his first look inside a reformatory after writing a few bad cheques. Peters realized he would have to straighten up and get smart if he was to stay bent and be successful. He began to read prodigiously; all this learning, he concluded, could be used to his advantage. Also, he would have to rid himself of the aura of the jailhouse and learn some manners. Peters left the young delinquent in the jailhouse, and emerged an affable rogue.

Peters began to pose as either someone well known, or as the relative of someone well known. Also, instead of cashing cheques at banks, he presented himself at stores and made purchases for which he would write a cheque, admitting that yes, he was Theodore Roosevelt II (the eldest son of President Theodore Roosevelt); or the son of Benjamin Franklin Trueblood, the general secretary of the American Peace Society; or head of the Geneva Convention. (Later, Peters would claim to be R.A. Coleman, an antique expert for the American Peace Society buying items for museum collections. He also impersonated the American Pulitzer Prize-winning novelist Booth Tarkington, among others.)

But the double hook in all this is that he only occasionally took the falsely obtained items away with him; usually he asked that they be delivered either to a fictitious address, or one belonging to the person whose identity he had assumed. As well, Peters always wrote the cheque for an amount that was just a little bit more than the cost of the item. In other words, if the suit cost $200, Peters would write a cheque for $225 and get $25 back from the clerk. By the time the matter came to the attention of the general secretary of the American Peace Society, Roosevelt II, or Woodrow Wilson's son-in-law, the worthy was usually inclined to forget the incident, not wanting the annoyance for such an insignificant amount.

So Peters went on his way for decades, crossing the United States posing as scores of people and writing scores of cheques, which he had to do to eke out a mildly comfortable living. He was jailed many times, but always returned to his old ways. When asked why, he once stated, "It would require the rock-like will of the Sphynx to resist such temptation." Sometimes he took a regular job, albeit with fake credentials. He was always outstanding in his straight employment, as if his job history were true. In the forties, for instance, Peters claimed to be a master printer, and was hired and worked for several years in that capacity.

When doing time, Peters was invariably well liked by both officials and fellow inmates. During one jolt at the McNeil Island Penitentiary in Washington State, Peters took over editorship of the prison newspaper, the *Island Lantern*, and developed it from a smudged, mimeographed rag to the number one prison paper in the United States. He became chief librarian and wrote to publishers requesting they donate books. Eventually, under his reign the library would possess fifteen thousand volumes, each selected by Peters. At McNeil Island he became the warden's chauffeur, and was allowed to live in a cottage on the grounds rather than in a cell. When his time was served, the whole prison population turned out for a farewell party and Warden Archer presented him with a watch. Peters left McNeil Island in 1931 and headed to downtown Seattle, where he immediately embarked on a shopping spree, billing everything to Archer before disappearing.

In 1952, a Frederick Emerson Peters was arrested by two FBI agents in a Washington, DC, hotel lobby after they recognized him as No. 22 on their Most Wanted list.

In 1959, Peters, registered as Dr. B.A. Morris, died of a heart attack in a New Haven, Connecticut, hotel room. He was seventy-four. In his personal effects, officials found several cheques made out to several people, as well as a used airline ticket in the name of Dr. Morton, and a train ticket from Oslo to Bergen in Norway for a J. Logan for the following week.

The FBI was called in, but couldn't figure out any of that.

Stephen Jacob Weinberg—alias Stanley Clifford Weyman, alias C. Sterling Weinberg, a.k.a. Royal St. Cyr, to name a few—was a Brooklyn street kid. Starting at an early age, he showed a penchant for dressing up. Later, he was seen to walk out the door as a soldier in the US Army, and return as an Arab prince. His neighbours thought he was merely eccentric. He left home one morning at age twenty, and sent his wife a letter three weeks later from Lima, Peru, where he had taken over the country's sanitation system. He made a small fortune on that one.

Weinberg was born in 1890, and died in 1960. Thus, he and Peters were contemporaries. When one thinks of these two characters—the mild-mannered and intellectual Peters, and the handsome and athletic Weinberg—making their living during the same era, one is inclined, depending on one's orientation, to be either mortified or elated. The thought of them combining their misguided talents brings to mind a Marx Brothers movie.

Even as a hustling urchin, it seems that Weinberg knew what the future held. He became an avid purchaser of clothes, with an emphasis on uniforms. In 1915, while still living with his parents, a notice in the newspaper caught his eye. The USS *Wyoming* had berthed at the Brooklyn Navy Yard. Weinberg searched through his closet and came up with an outfit that he thought was appropriate for a Romanian consular officer. Wearing his uniform, complete with admiral's hat, he left his house and went to the Navy Yard where he presented himself to the ship's captain as Lieutenant Ethan Allen Weinberg. He insisted that the sailors line up in formation so that he could conduct an inspection on behalf of the queen of Romania. He even went so far as to admonish individual sailors for flaws, real or imagined, in their uniforms or bearing. He got immense pleasure from returning salutes. Weinberg invited the ship's officers to dine as his guests that night at the Hotel Astor; the bill was to be sent to the Romanian Consulate. The dinner was underway and the wine flowing when detectives came to arrest him. As Weinberg was being led away, he was heard to tell one cop, "You could have at least waited until dessert."

Weinberg only served a couple of weeks in jail, after which he went on to his next outrageous caper. He paid a call at the 47th Regiment Armory in Brooklyn in the guise of Lieutenant Royal St. Cyr of the French Navy.

It was shortly thereafter that he put over the Peruvian caper, which lasted over a year.

Back in New York in 1921, he read that Princess Fatima Begum of Afghanistan had been snubbed by the American government, so Weinberg, using the name Weyman and wearing a white dress navy uniform, talked himself into the princess's suite, apologized for the government's oversight, and promised to secure for the princess a meeting with President Warren Harding. She gave him $10,000 to assist in his work. Your average con man would have walked away right then, but Weyman used some of the money to rent a private railway carriage for the princess and her entourage. In Washington, he got in to see Secretary of State Charles Evans Hughes and convinced him to set up a meeting with the president. There is Weyman in the newsreel shaking hands with Harding and patting him on the shoulder. They are seen smiling at each other; each probably knowing a fellow crook when he saw one.

Weinberg was then a US consul representative from Morocco, a Serbian military attaché, and a few other things before he went on to Hollywood to take over the arrangements for Rudolph Valentino's funeral, and become the personal physician for the heart throb's broken-hearted intended, Pola Negri. There he is in the newsreels again, *Zelig*-like, keeping away fans and reporters. When Negri was informed that Weinberg was a quack, she replied, "I don't care. He is the best doctor I've ever had."

As Clifford Weyman, he was for a time in the thirties an assistant to Viennese surgeon Adolf Lorenz, famous for treating crippled children. Weyman had convinced Lorenz he too was a surgeon.

In 1943, Weinberg was busted for running a school for draft dodgers, advising them of ways to get out of doing service. As he was being sentenced, Weinberg admitted he could not explain why he did these things: "The pattern of my life is not symmetrical," he told the judge. He was given his longest prison stretch, five years at the Atlanta Penitentiary. While there, he studied for a law degree and was admitted to the Georgia Bar.

When Weinberg was released from jail, he got a job as the New York correspondent for the *London Daily Mirror*. He worked in this capacity for two years before being exposed by another newspaper.

Weinberg got a job as a greeter at the famous Dinty Moore's Restaurant in Manhattan, run by Moore's daughter. He was so popular that Dorothy Moore kept offering him raises. He felt the need to confess his identity to her. She said, "That's fine, just don't let the customers know."

In 1960, Weinberg quit his job at the restaurant without explanation to take another as a night clerk at a motel in Yonkers that paid half the money. One evening two gunmen came in to rob the motel. Weinberg threw the cash box on the floor to distract the men, then jumped over the counter to attack them.

Weinberg had once told a judge that living just one life was boring. He had already lived several and, thus, had never been bored. All those lives ended that night in Yonkers as the gunmen shot him dead.

Charles Waterton
1782–1865

Charles Waterton spent only a few days in Canada, in 1824, visiting Quebec City, Montreal, and Niagara Falls. He never ventured west to southern Alberta, where there are lakes and a national park named for him. It was Thomas Blakiston, a surveyor with the Palliser Expedition, who did the naming. Blakiston respected the great explorers and naturalists of his time, and commemorated them with mountain peaks and ranges. Livingstone, Galton, and Gould —explorers all—had also never visited the places eventually named after them, but they were respectable sorts.

IMAGE: Charles Waterton by Charles Willson Peale, oil on canvas, 1824 (National Portrait Gallery, London). Used under license.

Officialdom, however, resented Waterton getting such an honour. He was, after all, a disreputable aristocrat who had wandered South America barefoot, travelling with blacks and Indians, sported the only "crewcut" of the age, was rumoured to bite dinner guests on the ankles, climbed trees to watch birds, was given to walking through his own mansion on his hands—a mansion where he spent most of his time not in one of the grand rooms, but in a tiny one in the attic, under the eaves, where he kept a full-sized and fully preserved baboon hanging from the ceiling, his own clothes hanging over a rope, and where he slept on the floor with a piece of wood for a pillow. This was a man described as "looking like a spider after a long winter," and who spoke as if he were simultaneously munching on a mouthful of walnuts.

Yes, Waterton was eccentric, but he was much more. His earliest biographer emphasized the oddity of his character and tried to minimize his achievements as a naturalist, but appeared more ridiculous than his subject because those very accomplishments were undeniable. Conversely, a contemporary biographer striving for seriousness, and wishing to concentrate on Waterton's scientific accomplishments, would be unable to keep her book from being leavened—and made more readable—by her subject's undeniable idiosyncrasies. There was no duality to Waterton's nature—no serious side independent of a nutty side—the complexities and contradictions made the man, and rendered him less eccentric than scalawagish.

Waterton was born in 1782. From his earliest days, he had an obsessive hatred of the common brown rat. His family had always been Catholic and Waterton was proud to have half a dozen saints in his family tree. A story was told in those days that when the Protestant William of Orange crossed the English Channel to oust the Catholic King James II, his ship was filled with brown rats that, upon landing, immediately set to decimating the native black rat population. The brown ones were imbued with the same self-righteous zeal as their Protestant shipmates. Such black rats as survived were forced into an underground existence. Most people took the story as metaphor, but not Waterton. This man, who after his youth never killed any other living creature, dedicated himself to eradicating brown rats. He concocted poison potions to kill them, and was seen swinging brown rats around by the tail before bashing their heads against trees.

Enrolled at a Catholic boarding school, he was soon expelled for climbing trees to watch birds (and for killing brown rats). At fourteen, he was sent to Stonyhurst College, a Jesuit school where the good fathers recognized his uniqueness and made him an official rat catcher. "The vermin disappeared by the dozen," he later boasted. After his formal schooling, Waterton went to Spain to stay with two uncles who had chosen to live in a Catholic country rather than be outcasts, like the black rats, in their native land. He wandered all about observing nature, particularly the quails that migrated from North Africa, and the apes of Gibraltar. Waterton learned Spanish, read Cervantes and became acquainted with Don Quixote, a man after his own heart.

In 1804, Waterton left on his first trip to British Guiana, ostensibly to manage his uncle's estates. His jungle wanderings were conducted part time for the first four years, after which he traversed the country full time for years, returning to England only now and again. He became interested in curare, the poison native Indians used on their arrows. He took different mixtures of the poison back to England and used them in experiments. Waterton would poison animals, and revive them by a method of ventilation using a bellows. He was thwarted in his attempts to try the potion on humans.

While in British Guiana, Waterton perfected a revolutionary method of taxidermy using bichloride of mercury. As well as preparing specimens for museums and private collections, including his own, he assembled mock animals—grotesques—often with satirical intent. Typical of the latter was a creature called "John Bull and the National Debt." It was a porcupine in a tortoiseshell with a human -like face, surrounded by snakes and lizards. Another, pieced together from the head of an owl, legs of a bittern, and wings of a partridge, was called "The Spirit of the Dark Ages, Unknown in England Before the Reformation." But most notorious of his creatures—known to some as "Waterton's Hallucinations"—was "The Nondescript," whose human-like face was made from the hindquarters of a howler monkey.

Waterton put a photograph of this creature in one of the editions of his most famous book, *Waterton's Wanderings in South America*, and many people assumed it to be a real animal that he had discovered in the jungle. When the truth got out, Waterton's reputation as a serious naturalist suffered immensely; he was not unduly disturbed. "The Nondescript" is still on display at the Wakefield Museum in England.

Returning to England from British Guiana, Waterton found himself famous because of his wanderings. Rant as he would against the Protestant establishment, he was offered a chance to be respectable by undertaking an exploration of Madagascar. He refused, and he'd never receive such an opportunity again. Later, he regretted his choice: "My commission was a star of the first magnitude... and the star went down below the horizon to appear no more."

Waterton was, however, greatly admired by the famous naturalist Sir Joseph Banks, who in his youth had sailed with Captain Cook, and in his old age, when Waterton knew him, was president of the Royal Society. Waterton's books were avidly read by the likes of Charles Dickens and Charles Darwin. His relations with some of the other famous naturalists of his time were tempestuous, to say the least. He met James Audubon in New York in 1824, and both men hated each other on sight. Waterton attacked him in print, and Audubon dismissed Waterton as "Charli that alligator riding gent" (the reference is to a well-known drawing of the time that showed the barefoot Waterton astride a cayman in British Guiana). Waterton also went after Paul Du Chaillu, who introduced the gorilla to Europe, calling the Frenchman's adventures in Africa "nothing but fables."

With the exception of trips to the Continent, Waterton spent the rest of his life at Walton Hall, the family's three-hundred-acre estate in Lancashire. In Bruges, Belgium, at 4:30 a.m. on May 11, 1829, Waterton, age forty-six, married the daughter of a friend from British Guiana. Anne Edmonstone was seventeen years old, half Arawak Indian, and had spent the night before her wedding at a convent in Bruges. Anne died in childbirth nine months later, and Waterton never got over his feeling of guilt. He brought Anne's two sisters, Helen and Eliza, from South America, and they remained with the naturalist until his death. They looked after his son, Edmund, and hosted the numerous dinner parties where Waterton might get up from the table to swing from the doorframes, or entertain his guests by scratching the back of his head with his foot.

Waterton built a three-mile-long, nine-foot-high stone fence around part of his estate, and turned it into one of the world's first nature reserves. He also continued his experiments with curare.

Waterton allowed no shooting on his property, which he opened up to visitors in the last years of his life. He paid six pence for every live hedgehog brought to his property, built different nesting places for different species of birds, and made commodious lairs for foxes. He convinced officials at the local lunatic asylum to allow inmates to come to his property. He let them wander and look through his telescopes. The upright citizens of the area deemed this activity proof of Waterton's own craziness; in our own time, we'd deem it excellent therapy.

Whenever Waterton heard of a freak of nature, be it a two-headed calf or a web-footed cat, he went to see it, or had its body sent to him. Likewise, he'd set off at a moment's notice to observe a human oddity. Giants, midgets, dwarves, and hydrocephalics were welcomed at Walton Hall, as were those with ichthyosis or hypertrichosis.

Forever wandering his property in shabby clothes, Waterton was often mistaken for a particularly unkempt groundskeeper, or recently released convict. In his later years, he was involved in lawsuits against the owner of a nearby soap manufacturing plant whom he sued for polluting the water and air for miles around. One suit led to another, with the manufacturer hoping that Waterton would just die. This he did in 1865—after the soapworks had been forced to move—just days before his eighty-third birthday, after a fall while escorting visitors across his property.

His son Edmund—who evinced absolutely none of the interests or predilections of his father—upon assuming control of Walton Hall, immediately threw his two aunts off the property, and after a season or two of hosting lavish dinners and allowing hunters to massacre the birds and animals, and running up massive debts, sold the house and land to the offending soap manufacturer.

Bata Kindai Amgoza ibn LoBagola 1877–1947

He called himself Bata Kindai Amgoza ibn LoBagola, and in the frontispiece to his 1930 autobiography, *LoBagola: An African Savage's Own Story*, he describes himself as "a black Jew, descended from the lost tribe of Israel, a savage who came out of the African bush into modern civilization and thenceforth found himself an alien among his own people and a stranger in the twentieth century world."

According to LoBagola, one day when he was nine years old (which would make it around 1896), he sneaked away from his village, located a three-day walk south of Timbuktu, and with a few friends journeyed to the sea. They had their first glimpse of white men when they paddled their canoe out to a ship anchored in the bay, and were welcomed on board. But after an hour or so, the ship drew anchor and began to move, and LoBagola's friends climbed overboard and started paddling the canoe, only to be capsized by huge waves and devoured by sharks. LoBagola, who had been poking around below deck, came up just in time to witness the catastrophe. As the ship sailed away, he became terrified and ran amok. Eventually the ship docked at Glasgow, and LoBagola jumped down onto the wharf, where he became quite the spectacle. He was rescued by a gentleman

IMAGE: Photo courtesy of the Penn Museum.

who brought him home. LoBagola lived for several years with the gentleman, his wife, and their son, who was about LoBagola's age. He learned to speak English and even attended school.

He was given passage back to Dahomey (now Benin) in West Africa. With his people again, LoBagola married and had children, but with a friend left once more for reasons he did not explain. They were attacked by murderous Fang people. After being rescued by the black guide for a party of British soldiers, LoBagola went to Ouidah and shipped back to Scotland. Jews in Glasgow made a fuss over him because he was from one of the Lost Tribes. After four years, he ran away and travelled to England, France, the Netherlands, Germany, and Latvia. In England, he got his first taste of show business, portraying a West African chief in Coventry's Lady Godiva parade.

There were several more trips between Europe and Africa, during which LoBagola underwent a series of harrowing adventures. He married a couple more times in Africa, fathered several more children, and killed a Dahomey warrior in a fight. "With his dying breath"—as LoBagola wrote many years later—the warrior cursed him, and "that curse followed me even to this day here in New York."

Not long after he arrived back in Scotland, the man who had first rescued him all those years ago died, leaving LoBagola an inheritance of £1,000. LoBagola travelled to London, where an astrologer stole his money, and to Liverpool, where he hooked up with a woman who ran a "travelling cinematograph show." LoBagola's job was to draw customers in by dancing and singing. The show owner also stole from him, but somehow LoBagola managed to get money for the passage across the Pond to Philadelphia. There he got work in a dime museum; dressed in skins and feathers, he danced, and gave talks on Africa. He also discovered he was able to put open flames to his skin without burning himself, or even feeling much pain. He billed himself as "The Fireproof Man," and told his audiences that this was a gift he learned from an old medicine man. His act was popular enough for LoBagola to graduate to theatres and the vaudeville circuit.

He left again for Africa, and in late 1911 in northern Nigeria he was flogged for not prostrating himself before a white man. He came down with malaria in Lagos, and when he recovered, he received passage to England, where he was robbed again. Some Nigerian friends paid for him to go back to America, where he got stage work because he had brought his "African dress" with him. After a few months, he was robbed yet again, and wound up shining shoes in a town in upstate New York when the First World War broke out.

LoBagola was assigned to the 38th Battalion of the Royal Fusiliers, a British regiment composed mainly of Jews. He served in Palestine and Egypt. With the war at an end, he was demobbed in England. There, the horse he'd bet on won the Derby, and he used his winnings to travel to Palestine to teach at a college in Jerusalem. Soon after, in Tanta, Egypt, LoBagola converted to Catholicism and taught at a Coptic school.

He eventually returned to Africa, but he immediately felt lost, so he travelled back to New York. He sought solitude in meditation at a monastery, but that only lasted a month. Next, he was an assistant at Fordham University for a month. He didn't quit, but rather "fell into trouble on the streets." This "trouble" got him a month in jail.

When released from jail, LoBagola worked five months in a factory, only to be fired when he asked for a raise. Destitute, he was hired to give a lecture on Africa at a public school in New York. "From that time, I have given many such talks," he wrote.

So ends the whirlwind record of his life experiences.

Throughout his harrowing story, LoBagola repeatedly refers to the subject of lying. Besides adventure and misfortune, lying is the main theme of his autobiography (with victimization being a sub-theme). As a teenager in Scotland, LoBagola "was on [his] way to being civilized, but [he] was not quite civilized enough to tell lies." And later, "I didn't know how to lie until I met white people... Here is where the science of a good lie saved me a lot of trouble." But just one page later, in the recounting of a folk tale, LoBagola has a wise old elephant declare that "a lie is never justified."

Well, Bata Kindai Amgoza ibn LoBagola was really Joseph Howard Lee, or so he claimed in 1934 when he was about to be deported to his supposed birthplace of Dahomey. He insisted he was born in 1887 at 620 Raberg Street in Baltimore, Maryland, the seventeenth child of Joseph Lee, a cook, and Lucy, a domestic servant.

In repudiating the story of his life to his interrogators, as given in his autobiography, "Mr. Lee" told what he called "the real truth" —a story that, although unverifiable, was accepted. This "real" story was filled with derring-do of another sort: the adventures of a merchant seaman roaming the seven seas and doing battle with injustice.

Actually, LoBagola was a street character who probably started out on one of those Baltimore corners made notorious in recent years by the HBO television series *The Wire*. Besides being a corner boy, "Joe Howard Lee" was a male hustler. It is true that he was a merchant seaman, and that he did see much of the world, including Africa. He was also an entertainer, and he lectured on Africa and its customs to audiences in Europe and America. He also appeared at several American universities, where he was taken seriously. His ability to con even African experts is indicated by his experiences in early 1911 at the University of Pennsylvania's Museum of Archaeology and Anthropology, where he lectured on African languages and cultures. His sponsor was Frank G. Speck, assistant curator of general ethnology at the museum, and later the founder of the anthropology department at Penn. Speck spoke with LoBagola/Lee at length, and recorded him on wax cylinders singing "authentic songs of his people." LoBagola's talks drew large crowds, and garnered good press notices. He was described as "by far the best exhibit at the Museum," and must have been quite the sight dressed in a native skirt, necklaces, and a headdress, parading through the galleries. *The Bookman* declared, "Those who have heard LoBagola speak realize that he is a master of the spoken tongue." Another magazine described him as "one of the greatest of platform entertainers."

The only traces remaining of this mysterious individual's life are found in a few letters exchanged with a booking agent, James B. Pond; some folders that attest to various vaudeville bookings;

and records from several prisons where he was incarcerated—usually for "sodomy" and "perversion"—for a total of thirteen years. One of the problems with his business correspondence is that many of the letters received by him bear a salutation to someone who is neither LoBagola, nor Joe, Joseph, Howard, or Lee. There is a "Dear Luke," for instance, and a just plain "Reese." One contract is signed "Alvin Johnson."

As for the origin of his African name, LoBagola probably cobbled it together from those of different African performers on European stages, such as Angazzo Bogolo, Beah Kindah, and Peter Lobengula.

But all these "proofs" are of the existence of someone calling himself Bata Kindai Amgoza ibn LoBagola. The certificate of naturalization he handed over to authorities was, of course, a fake. The birth certificate he provided was genuine, but was it LoBagola's? On the line where the name of the child was to be entered, there is only the notation "unnamed seventeenth child."

Throughout Black American songs, stories, fables, and folktales, there are trickster/hustler figures. The man calling himself LoBagola is one of these, only to an extreme.

But who he *really* was, nobody knows.

The remains of whomever he may have been occupy Plot 29 in the graveyard at Attica Prison (now the Attica Correctional Facility) in New York State.

LoBagola's assumed name, however, does live on amongst the lore of investors. In his "autobiography," LoBagola tells the story of an elephant stampede. The beasts rush through an area, and always return the same way. When there is a surge in the stock market that soon ceases and retreats—like a good old-fashioned speculative bubble—it's called a "LoBagola."

As for the man who called himself LoBagola, one doubts that his like will ever be seen again.

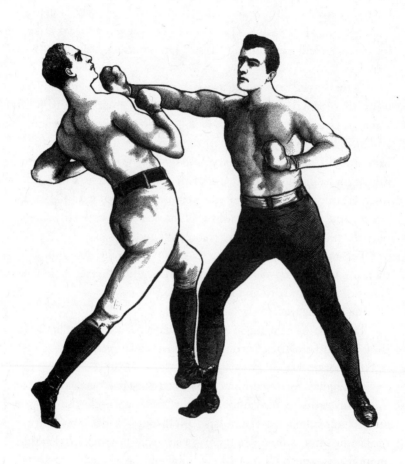

*"Boxing is like jazz in that most people
have no idea what's going on."*

—GEORGE FOREMAN, FORMER HEAVYWEIGHT CHAMPION

Two J.J.s and a Nick

There are plenty of things in the esoteric universe of professional boxing to mystify, confound expectations, and surprise the hell out of even the most cynical follower of the "sport." I put the word in quotations because one doesn't "play" boxing. It's so much more than a sport: it's a way of life. It is neither a middle-class pastime like baseball, nor something for the upper classes to do, like polo. As such, boxing is outside the norm and therefore attracts the best stories, the most interesting people, and by far the best literature. It also attracts prime examples of the genus Scalawag.

Boxing is its own universe, but what are the odds that any universe, no matter how vast, has turned out two characters, mirror images of each other, possessed of the same modus operandi and bearing the same names, first and last: James Johnston.

One hesitates to call their predilections unseemly, or their machinations dishonest; more apt is the designation of chicanery (or, in the words of a judge in New York, shaking his head over the exploits of the first J.J.: "One sees the glint in his eye and knows that his rascality must have its way. No real harm was done. Case dismissed").

After John Arthur "Jack" Johnson—not to be confused with our two J.J.s—became the first black man to win the heavyweight crown in 1908 (after "Huge Deal" McIntosh enticed him into the ring in Melbourne with a revolver) by knocking out the only Canadian champion in history, Tommy Burns, there arose throughout the world a frantic campaign to win back the title, then the ultimate symbol of masculinity, for the white race. It seems as if every saloon and circus strongman operation, every logging camp and boxing gym, in the white world was explored by hungry managers in fedoras.

A lot of bums showed up, were conquered, and went away. Just about the only people to profit by this craze were the managers, and none made out better than James Joy "Jimmy" Johnston, already known as "the Boy Bandit of Broadway."

Jimmy Johnston—our first J.J.—was born in Liverpool, England, in 1875, but came to America with his parents before the turn of the twentieth century. They settled in Hell's Kitchen in New York City. At age twelve, he was put to work in a foundry where he toiled for six years. When not at the foundry, he frequented a boxing gym and soon was engaging in amateur fights. He turned pro, but was astute enough to know he didn't have what it took to go anywhere as a pugilist. Consequently, he took to managing and promoting. He proved to be a natural and, eventually, became the matchmaker for Madison Square Garden.

Johnston joined the "great White Hope" hunt not long after Jack Johnson raised his gloves in victory. He didn't need a champion, just a fellow who'd make him some money. One day a guy from South Africa calling himself George "Boer" Rodel (whose real name was Lodewikus van Vuuren) walked into his office claiming to be a fighter. He had just crossed the Pond after suffering three straight knockouts. He told the Boy Bandit that it was all his manager's fault. Johnston sent him to the local gym but, alas, even the hangers-on were able to work him over. And that would have been the end of that story, but the Boy Bandit, as if to affirm his nickname, called up a local sports writer and gave him a big story about Rodel being a hero of the Boer War. The publicity, plus a string of hapless opponents, propelled his career. Johnston provided him with more set-ups, but soon the sports writers demanded Rodel fight a live opponent, thus he was matched with the number one white hope, Edward "Gunboat" Smith.

In those days, sports writers determined the winner of a fight, and they readily gave the decision to Smith, who had, after all, knocked

Rodel down ten times. One newsman, however, begged to differ; it was of no import that he hadn't even been at the fight. The scribe was the recipient, every now and again, of a sawbuck from Johnston.

The novelist and boxing writer Budd Schulberg wrote that Johnston "knew more angles than a geometry teacher."

Perhaps the height of Johnston's particular powers was revealed when he got Rodel a bout with Jess Willard, a.k.a. "the Pottawatomie Giant," the former champ who had knocked out Jack Johnson in 1915 for the heavyweight title. Willard was coming off a fight with a guy called Jack "Bull" Young who'd died under Willard's barrage of punches in 1913. Johnston gave Willard a story about Rodel's "heart condition"; one serious punch was liable to kill him. So Willard took it easy, and Rodel managed to get a decision.

Next, Johnston managed a fighter called "Agile" Andre Anderson, and put him in with a black fighter who suffered intensely from arthritis in his shoulders. Johnston paid the black fighter's corner men to dump ice water over his shoulders before the fight and between rounds. Not too long into the bout, the fighter began to shiver uncontrollably and was unable to raise his hands. Anderson got the decision, but his winning ways were not to continue. After several one-round knockouts, he drifted away from the game.

Johnston eventually got involved with a rich, old-money Philadelphia banker named Anthony Joseph Drexel Biddle, a boxing nut who had to be constantly dissuaded from getting in the ring himself. Walt Disney made a movie about Biddle, *The Happiest Millionaire*, starring Fred MacMurray.

(Johnston himself would later be portrayed on the big screen; Bruce McGill played him in the 2005 Ron Howard boxing movie *Cinderella Man*.)

At one point, Johnston became aware of the popularity of boxing in New York's Chinatown, and determined to cash in on it. He convinced an Irish fighter named Patrick Mulligan to get a soup-bowl haircut and dye his skin yellow. Immediately, Mulligan became Ah Chung, the lightweight champion of China.

Johnston was awarded the James J. Walker Award for Long and Meritorious Service to Boxing by the Boxing Writers Association of America in 1945. He died of heart failure on May 7, 1946, after attending a fight at St. Nicholas Arena.

If the contemporary James Johnston is not as well known as the old-timer, it is only because the second J.J. came along after the decline in boxing, which happened to coincide in North America with the mad rush to suburbia. Our second J.J. never had a big enough stage on which to strut his stuff. I knew him well in Vancouver, but of late I can get no information about him, his whereabouts, or if he is, indeed, still alive. Four years ago, I ran into the fight trainer Dave Cooke on Denman Street in Vancouver, who told me J.J. had been ill.

For several years from the mid-1980s to the mid-1990s, J.J. and I spent a lot time together; I mostly listened to his stories, which I was more than happy to do, and which he needed no encouragement to relate. He once got a telephone call from a matchmaker in Yugoslavia who asked him if he had a decent middleweight to bring over. At the time, J.J. was managing one Gordie Lawson. He told the man no problem, and asked the date of the fight. "Tomorrow," the Yugoslavian said.

When J.J. and his fighter arrived at the arena in Belgrade, no more than fifteen minutes late, they got a standing ovation from the crowd.

Like the first J.J., the younger Johnston had boxed. He dismissed his two pro fights as being "of no consequence."

He served in the merchant marine near the end of World War II and saw the world. When the war was over, he stayed on board and saw the world a few more times. Back in Vancouver, he published a boxing sheet called *Fistic Flashes*. In the early fifties, J.J. and some other people had what he called "a misunderstanding over some diamonds," and he went away for a year. On his return, he began to promote cards in places like Burnaby, Creston, and Nelson, BC. He soon became an agent dispatching boxers throughout North America and Europe. He often went with his charges. His fighters, more times than not, lost. He was investigated for ordering his fighters to take a dive, but J.J. swore to me that he never did such a thing, and I believed him if for no other reason than he took great delight in telling of his shenanigans, freely confessing that it was an impostor he dispatched to South Africa on a certain occasion. He once took a guy to Rotterdam who was not the weight the contract stipulated. J.J. and the promoter spent a couple hours before the weigh-in sewing lead weights into the fighter's trunks.

Another time, he brought a Vancouver fighter named Jerry "Mack Truck" Reddick to Amsterdam. He had Reddick get on a scale at Schiphol. Reddick was supposed to be 170, "give or take a pound," but he was only 165. There being no stores open that sold lead weights in Amsterdam that day, J.J. picked up a rock and had his fighter stick it in his athletic supporter before the weigh-in.

J.J. had a thousand and one stories, many of them seemingly tall tales unless you knew the man. One Saturday night I found myself without a date to a party in the Kitsilano area of Vancouver. The hosts were wealthy, as were most of the guests. I was invited as a curiosity. My date had reneged, but I was obligated to bring someone. I ran into J.J. on the street and enlisted him as my "date." As we were walking to the door, threading our way between the Mercedes and Bentleys, I began to doubt my snap decision. I feared that he'd fit in even less than me. But inside, after being distracted for a while, I wondered where J.J. was and what he was doing with this bunch. I located him in the middle of a white leather couch, flanked by women, with five or six men literally at his feet. He was telling a story—one that I'd heard before—about being in a jail cell in a town in Wyoming, sentenced to ten days.

"I was bored out of my mind," J.J. was saying. "There was an old guy who came in to sweep the floor every day. When he didn't show up one time, the sheriff told me he was taking a few days off with the flu. I asked to be allowed to sweep the floor because I was so bored. Now it had not escaped my notice that, it being August, the door to the street was left open. Well, I swept the floor that first day, the sheriff watching my every move. Same the second day, and the one after that. After the fourth day, the sheriff wasn't paying attention to me. I always did a good job and put the broom back in the right place. On the seventh day, I was sweeping dirt toward the front door; the sheriff wasn't looking and away I went."

There was a guy sitting near J.J. who smirked, saying, "What a load of B.S. You really expect us to believe that?"

J.J. shrugged. "Well," he said, "do you want to place a bet on whether it's true or not?"

"Sure. Do you have any money?" the fellow asked condescendingly.

J.J. dipped into his hip pocket and came up with three double sawbucks and laid them on the floor at the guy's feet. After the fellow matched them, J.J., still holding his wallet, extracted a clipping from the daily newspaper of the town where he had been incarcerated. "Inmate Sweeps Himself Out of Jail" the headline read. The story went on to relate how James J. Johnston, a wily, long-time criminal from Canada, caused a heap of embarrassment to the town's sheriff by...

So we left that party with sixty dollars more than we had upon arrival. Mr. Johnston stood me to a late dinner at a Greek restaurant on Fourth Avenue.

J.J. liked to tell me about all the characters he'd met in boxing. I asked him who the most interesting one was. "Nick Zubray," he said without hesitation. I had heard of the notorious "Mayor of Tap City"; who hadn't in those circles? Everyone in Canada with the remotest connection to boxing knew about "Nick's luck." Bad luck is having a fight card snowed out. "Nick's luck" is having a fight card snowed out in July. (Once, Nick promoted a six-bout program that resulted in six first-round knockouts.)

I met Nick Zubray only twice, unfortunately. I visited him in his hideout one winter at the Hotel Macdonald in Edmonton and, true to all the stories, he was dressed in a white suit with a pink carnation pinned to his lapel, and yes, he poured us glasses of pink champagne. He had several suitcases piled by the door, as if he was about to depart on a long trip. Mario Lanza was playing in the background on a portable record player. When the side ended, Nick filled the silence with his own arias. He had a good voice, too.

A bull-necked man with a battered face, Nick's hands were broad and his fingers manicured. He talked an old-time hustler's language full of "tap cities," "ankle expresses," gaffs, and grifts, and he worked in a four or five syllable word every chance he got—describing, for instance, getting punched in the head once, causing him to have a "vertiginous sensation."

We first hit it off over opera, rather than boxing, he being curious about me growing up in the same neighbourhood in Philadelphia as Mario Lanza. We had a good-natured spat over the relative merits of Enrico Caruso and Beniamino Gigli (I was a Gigli man). But pretty soon we were cutting up touches, or he was.

People insist that in money matters, Nick Zubray was unfailingly honest. For example, he once lived for an entire year in Vancouver's Mayfair Apartment Hotel. One morning he took "French leave," owing the hotel $10,000—a dastardly thing to do, but he came back a year later and, before an astonished desk clerk, peeled off one hundred one-hundred-dollar bills.

J.J. told me that when he was himself down on his uppers, Nick hired him to put up promotion posters for a fight and overpaid him. The next time they met, Nick was tap city and J.J. lent him fifty bucks. A month later Nick was back in Vancouver, invited J.J. to dinner, picked up the tab, and handed his pal a box with a pair of brand new shoes inside. When J.J. looked puzzled, Nick shrugged. "Well, I remembered we took the same size and I don't want them."

It is doubtful we will ever see Nick's like again. Doubtful? No, impossible.

In his recently published autobiography, George Chuvalo declares, "I loved Zube."

In 1983, Nick fell down on the street and didn't beat the count. Even in that condition, he was more alive than most others walking around.

And it's even more true now.

Top Left: Bea Miles, barefoot, speaking with reporters, c. 1946. Gordon King, State Library of NSW.

Centre: Alex the Holy; photo by Randy Glenhill. Courtesy of the author.

Bottom Left: Cowboy at the intersection of Queen and Bathurst Streets in Toronto, circa 1977. Photo by Tom Skudra.

Rascal Street

If I lament the passing of genuine scalawags from the world scene, I have at least come to accept this sad state of affairs and the reasons for it. The world has become homogenized; people and emotions reified; your phones are tapped; Obama's reading your email; and surely right this minute there is a camera pointed at you. I have ceased to rant and rave about it, but what does rankle me and what I cannot accept is the near absolute disappearance of interesting street life in big cities, particularly those in Canada, my country whose streets I know best.

I am not talking about the homeless, crazy or not, but am referring to the walking monuments to eccentricity who added colour to the avenues and boulevards, who were sparks to the Big Smoke. The heyday of these characters, in Toronto anyway, was the 1970s, a decade that was also my heyday in that city, a fact that is purely coincidental but for which I am thankful. The city was too conservative in prior decades of the twentieth century—stultifying decades in the tight grip of Victorianism—and too conservative in subsequent decades once gentrification came to reign and colonize. In the late sixties, things suddenly opened upward and outward. It was as if a crack appeared in the grey sidewalk and bright flowers burst forth and shook their petals.

Perhaps it was the same in Vancouver or Edmonton. I remember my very first evening in Vancouver in June, 1970. I had hitchhiked

across the country in just five days, breezing right through notorious Wawa, though my luck ran out in New Westminster, BC, and
I had to catch a local bus. No sooner did I alight downtown and
look around, than I saw a trim woman of about forty years of age
come walking along Georgia Street with her back bent as far back-
ward as it was possible for one to bend. Her head was also tilted
back, and she was staring at the sky. I watched her walk for a block
and she never changed her posture or moved her head, somehow
negotiating the crowds by a kind of internal radar. I noticed the
woman a couple of days later. In fact, I saw her just about every time
I came to Vancouver, well into the 1980s. I learned that she was
notorious and the object of numerous stories: "Her boyfriend was
a pilot and he was shot out of the sky during the war"; "Her boyfriend got on a plane for Hong Kong and never came back"; "Her
children died in a fire and she's looking for them in heaven." I used
to fret that this last tale was true.

There was another woman in Vancouver, in late middle age when
I first encountered her, who lived somewhere out west on Georgia
Street, on the border between downtown and the West End, and was
always dressed to the nines, albeit in a late-forties manner. She'd often
wear a cloche cap with a veil, high heels and, around her neck, a
wrap made of a marten or fisher. She had big eyes, powdered her
face white, had a black beauty mark, and a large goitre on the left
side of her neck. The goitre was huge when I saw her for the first
time in the mid-seventies, and it just got bigger. She always glanced
at me sort of sideways and up from under the swelling with a sad,
resigned expression. I last saw her in about the year 2000, at which
time the goitre was nearly as large as her head.

There was an old-time organ grinder with a skittish monkey
whose post was outside the train station on Powell Street. I saw the
pair twice in the early seventies, but never again. Maybe age had
caught up with them. There was a man I encountered in Vancouver
and Toronto so many times that we became, if not friends, more
than acquaintances. He called himself Nat Goldwater, and we met
on the beach at English Bay the day of the Ali vs. Ellis boxing
match in 1971. He was walking along the beach with a portable

radio on his shoulder and smoking a cigar. He was at least twenty-five years older than me, and looked like the kind of guy who would be listening to the fight, so I called to him. It turned out that he was listening to the horse races at Hastings Racecourse in Exhibition Park. He came over and sat down near my friend and I, and we soon were buddies. In fact, when my friend and I were going to head back east, having bought an old Dodge from two young guys for thirty-five dollars—they said they were selling it so cheap because they just had to buy some grass—Nat came along with us. In Calgary, he said he knew the publisher of the *Herald* newspaper, and it turned out that he did; I went with him up to the executive offices and the big man slipped Nat fifty bucks.

We dropped Nat off in Winnipeg, and the next time I saw him was an evening a couple of years later in Toronto. He was selling newspapers from a stand on Gould Street near Yonge. Often when he got a rare-looking coin, he'd examine it and might bring out a greasy, twisted paperback guide to coin prices. I found him doing just that. "Always got an angle, eh, Nat?"

"Yeah, Jimmy," he replied casually, as if we'd just seen each other around the time the early edition hit the streets. "A guy's got to."

I'd see him now and again in Toronto, and he always seemed to be on the skids; he was becoming an old guy who lived in the past. One time he produced a shoebox of black and white photos. "Here we are, Mimi and me at the Copa... This one is me, and you probably recognize the other guy, Jack Dempsey."

But then in the late eighties, there he was on Davie Street in Vancouver, all dressed up in a sharp suit, with styled hair, smoking a big cigar, and getting into a limousine. "I told you I was working on something big. Come by the Hilton tomorrow. Ask for me at the desk," he said when he saw me.

I couldn't make it for a couple of days, by which time Nat had departed. The hotel clerk told me "Mr. G." had gone to the airport to catch his flight to Bermuda.

The last time I saw Nat was at a garage sale—my garage sale—in Kelowna, BC. He was with a woman younger than me.

How he knew I was in Kelowna or, for that matter, having a

garage sale, was never revealed. He said he'd made a lot of money and lost most of it. The last thing he said was that they were on their way to Nelson, BC. I never saw or heard from him again.

Kelowna was also the last place I ever saw a notorious street character who called himself Ed Chameleon.

I had first met Ed one morning in Toronto when I was awoken by an unusual noise in my apartment. I opened my eyes and there was a man who looked like a Jewish-Indian gangster leaning over me and telling me I was "on the Right Path." He certainly hadn't been there when I went to bed the previous night, nor had I ever seen him before.

"How did you get in?" I asked.

"By the fire escape. You really should lock your window. Now very few people are on the Right Path."

"Why don't you go into the kitchen and make some coffee."

"Okay, where is it?"

"Out the door and to the right."

We became friends, but I never found out his real name.

Ed was fifty years old and had been very wealthy—the basis of his fortune being a business that guaranteed to deliver to you anywhere in the five boroughs of New York City a hot steak, chicken, or ribs dinner within forty-five minutes, or your money back. He had invested much of his earnings in real estate and was flying high, a real tycoon, until he met Leslie, a post-beatnik, pre-hippy girl who turned him on to grass and then LSD, which they pursued wholeheartedly.

Eventually Ed was declared incompetent to manage his money, and given a monthly pension. He and Leslie fled New York for Toronto. He was solid enough to handle the daily doses of acid, but Leslie was completely gone. She might have been attractive had she done something with her hair and bathed now and again. She wore skimpy dresses and was usually barefoot. Ed told me he always made sure she left the house with shoes on, but by noon they had usually been left somewhere along the way. He had taken to calling at second-hand stores and buying the cheapest shoes he could find for her, ten or fifteen pairs at a time.

So picture the two of them on the summer streets of Toronto in 1970: Ed with grey hair combed straight back, a wise street-corner cynic's expression on his face, in a leather jacket; and lank-haired Leslie, her wide eyes blinking—the sort of deep blinks that always reminded me of someone gulping water from a fountain and taking a deep breath after every swallow. They would go down the streets, Ed closely regarding the bumpers and side-view mirrors of automobiles, and Leslie taking in the gob-smacking wonder of asphalt and mortar between bricks.

Leslie liked to go into supermarkets and stare at the pretty colours of the merchandise on display. I swear that I once saw her in the cereal section of a store at Robert and Bloor in the Annex, where she was stroking a box and cooing, "Oooh, Tony. Tony Tiger, I love you."

She was finally banned from the store. The general manager, produce manager, clerks, and cashiers would sometimes have to chase her up and down the aisles. She'd knock boxes off the shelves to slow their pursuit, or else bend forward from the waist and lift her dress for the benefit of the stock boys.

Ed wrote a play, *The Universal Sea,* the theme being that the world was a big ocean and we were all fish swimming around in it. Ed walked around the streets singing "It's me; it's me—just another little fish in the universal sea."

There were maybe ten characters or fish in Ed's play—all people he knew from the streets—and I was one of them: the Tuna. He was the wise, old Dolphin. It was a lot of fun; no one on stage had any idea of what he or she was doing, especially Leslie who was a sleek Marlin. Fifteen years later in Vancouver, I was walking in the laneway between Hastings and Pender near the old Orange Door, when a guy looked up from his exploration of a dumpster and greeted me. I nodded. "Oh, man! Don't you remember me? I was the Mackerel."

I saw Ed Chameleon for the last time in 1992 in the washroom of a restaurant on Bernard Street in Kelowna. He was looking terribly old and diminished. His pants were held up with a length of rope. He acknowledged me with the slightest of smiles, but his eyes

were bleary and dull. I asked where he was going. "East," he said.
As he was leaving, he added, "Leslie died."

There were so many others in those days, like Cowboy, who
hung around the intersection of Queen and Bathurst in Toronto
walking his three-speed English bicycle that was all tarted up with
plastic streamers on the handle grips and a generator operated by
pedal power. Cowboy wore boots, western slacks, satin cowboy
shirts, and a ten-gallon hat; he was an Indian. He also exchanged
greetings with the father and son who owned the hardware store
on the south side of Queen, just west of Bathurst. They had match-
ing pot bellies. In warm weather, these two sat outside on folding
aluminum beach chairs like a couple of sallow beach balls. The son
looked like a very old man, and liked to say to me, gesturing to his
father with a thumb, "He's a war veteran. Tell 'em, Dad, what war
you fought in."

"Boer War," his father said, and it was true.

Another fixture on the streets of Toronto was a guy known as Alex
the Holy, who sold postcards and was often to be seen "grounded"
to a parking meter or other metal pole. This, he said, was in order to
replace negative energy accumulated during his commercial rounds.
Some old-timers called him Rosie, which I couldn't figure. And it
was not as if you could ask him either, all direct questions being
answered with grim stares. Yet if he was of a mind, he could talk
your ear off. My friend Nick Drumbolis who worked at a Mob-run
pornographic bookstore on Yonge Street, informed me that the nickname of Rosie for the man nicknamed Alex the Holy, dated from
the 1950s when he sold roses at the Yonge-Bloor subway entrance.
Nick knows all the street characters of times past, as well as who
really wrote Shakespeare's plays. Alex, he informs me, was a Hungarian refugee named Alex Tonelli.

But I do not believe, as does Nick, that Alex the Holy was actually Fabian Lloyd, nicknamed Arthur Cravan.

There was a young man who frequented the side streets off lower
Yonge, where he'd sit on the curbs and masturbate, his only conces-

sion to modesty being the tails of the overcoat he wore. The locals were used to him, and ignored his onanistic activity.

And then there was Norman Elder, who deserves a book to himself. One of the first people I met in Toronto—if not the first—he owned the Norman Elder Gallery on Bay Street one block north of Bloor on the east side. What he showed were mostly his own paintings: great primitive oils. He came from a wealthy family, and had competed in two Olympics on the Canadian equestrian team. He told me he had burned down his neighbour's barn on Park Lane Circle when he was eight years old. He used to spend his allowance going to the Arctic, New Guinea, or the Amazon, and living with the native people, all before he was out of his teens. He quit his architecture studies at the University of Toronto the day before graduation. He kept a few snakes in the Bay Street gallery, but that was nothing compared to what awaited guests at the house on Bedford Road that he moved into a few years later. But before he moved there, he could often be seen walking down Bay Street carrying a spear in one hand, and a leash in the other to which a pig was attached.

Norman once called me up and invited me to come by the gallery at noon. When I showed up, he was with a beautiful Italian woman who had a camera around her neck and a camera bag over her shoulder. He told her, gesturing at me, "Jim knows Toronto. He'll take you around."

The woman and I spent the day visiting my favourite places in the city. She turned out to be Gina Lollobrigida.

One night I saw Norman on television taking a bath in a canvas camp tub, singing and whistling. It was a bug spray commercial.

He was president of the Canadian chapter of the Explorers Club, and his Bedford Road house was filled with pythons and shrunken heads, stuffed wildebeests, spears, shields, paintings, and statuary.

Before he got a Lincoln Town Car with venetian blinds in the back window, Norman had a 1962 Ford at which he had flung hundreds of clumps of epoxy, and painted chocolate brown. One afternoon a cop pulled Norman's Ford over on Parliament Street. I was in the passenger's seat.

"Gee, officer, I wasn't doing anything wrong, was I?" Norman asked.

"No," said the cop. "I just wanted to get a closer look at your car." After a moment, the cop said, "You guys know what this car looks like, right?"

We nodded, but he told us anyway: "It looks like a long piece of shit."

And then there was Miss Sweden, who would commandeer a piece of the pavement to preach social democracy, sometimes in English. She was of a certain age, had bleach-blond hair, a ready smile, and wore a tiara, a satin halter top, harem pants, Turkish slippers, and necklaces of found objects. She always reminded me of one of the Gabor sisters. I assumed she had rooms somewhere in the Annex because I would see her on Bloor between Spadina and Bathurst, so I was, therefore, shocked to encounter her one day at the crepuscular hour walking down the Danforth near Pape, wrapped in a chenille bedspread.

When I moved back to Toronto after twenty-four years in the west, the very first day in the city I saw a pair of Sri Lankans with a bicycle at the corner of Bathurst and Bloor. The one riding the bicycle had just pulled over to the curb at the northwest corner. His legless companion, who was laughing maniacally, was on a roller board; he had lost his grip on the ropes that attached him to the fender of the bike, and had hit the curb ten yards back. The driver got off the bike, took in the situation, and he too began laughing uproariously.

I continued walking west on Bloor and just past Ossington Avenue on the south side of the street spied a dwarf coming toward me. He was smoking a cigar and wearing a T-shirt with horizontal red and white stripes, baggy black jeans, and a Greek fisherman's cap. When he saw me, he touched the brim of his cap and smiled.

If you never encountered any of these characters, more's the pity. They enhanced the street. Unfortunately you can't look them up, because in Canada there is, in addition to the grim facts that render most of them obsolete, no interest in recording the presence of such people. They flowered for a brief moment, and wilted. In other countries—England, France, and Australia, particularly—there are entire books about such urban fauna.

In Australia in recent times, there was a man named Arthur Stace who wandered Sydney scrawling "Eternity" on buildings and sidewalks. Raised by alcoholic parents, gassed in the First World War, blinded in one eye, Stace had an excuse to hit the bottle himself. It was following a religious conversion that he took to Eternity. He scribbled and scrawled for nearly thirty years before being discovered. There is a movie and a radio play about Stace, and he was celebrated at the Sydney Olympics in 2000.

And then there was Beatrice (Bea, or Bee) Miles, whose upbringing was as privileged as Arthur Stace's was unfortunate. Raised in an upper-middle-class suburb, educated at private schools and universities, Bea was tall and good looking, and at age twenty took to riding around Sydney on a bicycle in a ball gown while blowing a whistle. She would stop her bike and jump on the hoods of cars and taxis. For this, and her notions of women's rights and sexual freedom, her father put her in an "insane asylum." Upon her release—the result of an active campaign in her favour by the press—Bea did more of the same, only more so. Bea jumped into taxis or on to streetcars and refused to pay fares. One driver who she did pay in 1955 was a female who took her from downtown Sydney to downtown Perth, and back. The ride cost Bea £600, and took nineteen days.

In her thirties, Bea took to living on the streets, sleeping in parks and tunnels. She devoted several hours each day to reading in public libraries.

She had memorized a good bit of Shakespeare—all the sonnets and great speeches in the plays—and she would take requests, asking only a few coins for a recitation.

Bea was a great swimmer, and probably the first woman to swim across the shark-infested waters of Bondi Bay, which she did with a knife strapped to her leg. One time when a trolley driver refused to carry her unless she paid the fare, Bea kicked him off and drove the trolley to the beach, picking up riders along the way and dropping them off. She got into a fist fight with a Bondi lifeguard because he wouldn't allow her to bring her pet sheep on the beach.

She died in 1973 at the Little Sisters of the Poor Home for the Aged, having told the sisters: "I have no allergies...one complex, no delusions, two inhibitions, no neuroses, three phobias, no superstitions and no frustrations." She was seventy-one.

At her funeral, they played "Waltzing Matilda" and "Tie Me Kangaroo Down, Sport."

There is now a homeless shelter named after her. There is a play about her, and several stories and novels, including Kate Grenville's *Lillian's Story*, which was made into a movie in 1995.

Now, of course, the grim realities of modern life militate against the flourishing of street life. Indeed, against the very existence of it. People no longer seem to want to hang out on the streets, or go *flâneur*ing. Why should they, when they have the world in one hand, and can access any and all parts of it with a couple of nimble thumb strokes? People don't know the couple next door, but have Facebook friends in Sulawesi.

It's not just the fault of historians, local or otherwise, that street life has evaded celebration, or even acknowledgement, in Canadian literature. (There is Hugh Garner—the British-born Canadian novelist—and...well, there must be someone else, but the exceptions are few.) Not even hipsters and bohemians have dabbled in the world of street life and given it their particular coat of irony, and reifying "characters"—or what they condescendingly call "hoboes." At least that would indicate they noticed.

The reason for this is not exactly a mystery. Our official literature from the beginning has been solidly middle class, buttressed by Puritanism. The street is something unseemly. It's all right to teach Balzac and Dickens, Catullus and Villon (who am I kidding?), but don't dare ape their subject matter. (Speaking of apes, just imagine what would happen if an organ grinder with a monkey set up on a street corner these days. There'd be animal control services, public health inspectors—the poor guy would be hauled in for multiple offences, including whatever terrorist legislation they could trot out.)

We do not regard street life, as do Europeans and most everyone else, as merely Life. Sitting on our front steps (and not back steps) is just not done here. It is so *lower* class. Oh, those horrible sights: the laughing, shouting, carousing, music blaring from cranked-up car stereos, and, yes, screaming, shouting, and fighting—all that loving and hating. All that *living*. No one wants to see some lady walking by, back bowed as she peers into the sky. Well, at least she doesn't have a goitre on her neck the size of a rainforest mushroom!

These are our grim realities, and it can only get worse. When a kid starts out on "play dates," what else can be expected? The only problem I encounter on the street these days is when someone using a cellphone bumps into me. They always look dazed: What's this? Oh, God! An actual person. Real life!

"You're out on the streets looking good," sang Ms. Joplin. Not bloody likely.

I'm not bemoaning the long-gone past. I'm lamenting the recent one, with all those people—like Nat, Ed, Cowboy; that dwarf in the Greek fisherman's cap; the whiskey priest who'd given up the Church for the religion of jazz, and stopped in the middle of "How High the Moon" to offer me a slug from the pint of rye in his tenor sax case—I'll never see again.

Grenville commented that Bea Miles "wrote her own story on the blank pages of her city." That's what all these people—these scalawags—have done; but since in Canada we don't appreciate such individuals, the same way we don't appreciate much of our history—the most interesting part—their stories have faded, or are fading, from the book of the street, leaving only blank pages.

About the Author

Jim Christy is a writer, artist, and tireless traveller. The author of over thirty books, including collections of poetry and short stories, novels, travel writing, and biography, his journeys have taken him from the Yukon to the Amazon, Greenland to Cambodia. He has covered wars, and exhibited his art internationally. Raised in inner-city Philadelphia, he moved to Toronto when he was twenty-three years old and became a Canadian citizen at the first opportunity. His most recent books are, *Bad Day for Ralphie* (stories), and the poetry work *The Big Thirst and other Doggone Poems*. A resident of British Columbia's Sunshine Coast for many years, he currently lives in Belleville, Ontario.

Photo by John Hamley